OPPOSING VIEWPOINTS® SERIES

Medical Technology

Carol Ullmann and Lynn M. Zott, Book Editors

GREENHAVEN PRESS
A part of Gale, Cengage Learning

GALE
CENGAGE Learning·

Detroit • New York • San Francisco • New Haven, Conn • Waterville, Maine • London

GALE
CENGAGE Learning®

Elizabeth Des Chenes, *Director, Publishing Solutions*

© 2013 Greenhaven Press, a part of Gale, Cengage Learning

Gale and Greenhaven Press are registered trademarks used herein under license.

For more information, contact:
Greenhaven Press
27500 Drake Rd.
Farmington Hills, MI 48331-3535
Or you can visit our Internet site at gale.cengage.com.

For product information and technology assistance, contact us at:

Gale Customer Support, 1-800-877-4253.
For permission to use material from this text or product, submit all requests online at www.cengage.com/permissions.

Further permissions questions can be emailed to permissionrequest@cengage.com.

Articles in Greenhaven Press anthologies are often edited for length to meet page requirements. In addition, original titles of these works are changed to clearly present the main thesis and to explicitly indicate the author's opinion. Every effort is made to ensure that Greenhaven Press accurately reflects the original intent of the authors. Every effort has been made to trace the owners of copyrighted material.

Cover image © lucadp/Shutterstock.com.

LIBRARY OF CONGRESS CATALOGING-IN-PUBLICATION DATA

Medical technology / Carol Ullmann and Lynn M. Zott, book editors.
        pages cm. -- (Opposing viewpoints)
    Includes bibliographical references and index.
    ISBN 978-0-7377-6058-3 (hardcover) -- ISBN 978-0-7377-6059-0 (pbk.)
1. Medical technology. 2. Medical innovations. I. Ullmann, Carol, editor of compilation. II. Zott, Lynn M. (Lynn Marie), 1969- editor of compilation.
    R855.3.M424 2013
    610.284--dc23
                                                                        2012040690

Printed in the United States of America
1 2 3 4 5   17 16 15 14 13

Contents

Chapter 1: Does Medical Technology Provide Better Patient Outcomes?

Chapter 2: How Does Medical Technology Affect Health-Care Costs?

Chapter 3: How Do Electronic Medical Records Impact Patients?

Why Consider
Opposing Viewpoints?

> *"The only way in which a human being
> can make some approach to knowing
> the whole of a subject is by hearing
> what can be said about it by persons of
> every variety of opinion and studying
> all modes in which it can be looked at
> by every character of mind. No wise
> man ever acquired his wisdom in any
> mode but this."*
>
> John Stuart Mill

In our media-intensive culture it is not difficult to find differing opinions. Thousands of newspapers and magazines and dozens of radio and television talk shows resound with differing points of view. The difficulty lies in deciding which opinion to agree with and which "experts" seem the most credible. The more inundated we become with differing opinions and claims, the more essential it is to hone critical reading and thinking skills to evaluate these ideas. Opposing Viewpoints books address this problem directly by presenting stimulating debates that can be used to enhance and teach these skills. The varied opinions contained in each book examine many different aspects of a single issue. While examining these conveniently edited opposing views, readers can develop critical thinking skills such as the ability to compare and contrast authors' credibility, facts, argumentation styles, use of persuasive techniques, and other stylistic tools. In short, the Opposing Viewpoints Series is an ideal way to attain the higher-level thinking and reading skills so essential in a culture of diverse and contradictory opinions.

In addition to providing a tool for critical thinking, Opposing Viewpoints books challenge readers to question their own strongly held opinions and assumptions. Most people form their opinions on the basis of upbringing, peer pressure, and personal, cultural, or professional bias. By reading carefully balanced opposing views, readers must directly confront new ideas as well as the opinions of those with whom they disagree. This is not to argue simplistically that everyone who reads opposing views will—or should—change his or her opinion. Instead, the series enhances readers' understanding of their own views by encouraging confrontation with opposing ideas. Careful examination of others' views can lead to the readers' understanding of the logical inconsistencies in their own opinions, perspective on why they hold an opinion, and the consideration of the possibility that their opinion requires further evaluation.

Evaluating Other Opinions

To ensure that this type of examination occurs, Opposing Viewpoints books present all types of opinions. Prominent spokespeople on different sides of each issue as well as well-known professionals from many disciplines challenge the reader. An additional goal of the series is to provide a forum for other, less known, or even unpopular viewpoints. The opinion of an ordinary person who has had to make the decision to cut off life support from a terminally ill relative, for example, may be just as valuable and provide just as much insight as a medical ethicist's professional opinion. The editors have two additional purposes in including these less known views. One, the editors encourage readers to respect others' opinions—even when not enhanced by professional credibility. It is only by reading or listening to and objectively evaluating others' ideas that one can determine whether they are worthy of consideration. Two, the inclusion of such viewpoints encourages the important critical thinking skill of objectively evaluating an author's credentials and bias. This evaluation will illuminate an author's reasons for taking a particular stance on an issue and will aid in readers' evaluation of the author's ideas.

It is our hope that these books will give readers a deeper understanding of the issues debated and an appreciation of the complexity of even seemingly simple issues when good and honest people disagree. This awareness is particularly important in a democratic society such as ours in which people enter into public debate to determine the common good. Those with whom one disagrees should not be regarded as enemies but rather as people whose views deserve careful examination and may shed light on one's own.

Thomas Jefferson once said that "difference of opinion leads to inquiry, and inquiry to truth." Jefferson, a broadly educated man, argued that "if a nation expects to be ignorant and free . . . it expects what never was and never will be." As individuals and as a nation, it is imperative that we consider the opinions of others and examine them with skill and discernment. The Opposing Viewpoints Series is intended to help readers achieve this goal.

David L. Bender and Bruno Leone,
Founders

Introduction

> *"Technology provides an increasing ability to monitor, prevent, diagnose, control, and cure a growing number of health conditions and to improve quality and length of life. Questions remain, however, about how much innovation and improvement in new and existing technologies is possible when resources are constrained and health care expenditures are rising to unacceptable levels, about the opportunity costs of using one technology versus another (or neither), and whether target populations are appropriately and equitably served."*
>
> National Center for Health *Statistics,* Health, United States, 2009: With Special Feature on Medical Technology, *January 2010.*

Medical technology is any tool used to solve a medical problem, ranging from a simple Band-Aid to a cardiac defibrillator. As health care has become more complex, solving medical problems has led to ethical and financial issues. One major ethical issue that involves medical technology is keeping people alive regardless of the quality of their lives. A major financial issue involving medical technology concerns companies that seek to make money from their devices or treatments, regardless of the relative quality of care.

Medical technology has enabled health-care professionals to treat more people with better results. As a result, people are living longer and mortality rates are low in the industrialized world. For example, in the United States, mortality dropped 60 percent between 1935 and 2010, according to a 2012 data brief from the National Center for Health Statistics. In 2006 the Congressional Research Service reported that life expectancy had nearly doubled since 1900, from forty-eight years for women and forty-six years for men, to eighty years for women and seventy-five years for men in 2003.

Some of the technologies that have improved quality of life include laparoscopic surgery, coronary stents, and Cesarean-sections (C-sections). Laparoscopic, or keyhole, surgery uses smaller incisions, which leads to less pain and faster recovery from abdominal surgery than traditional open surgery methods, but there is a small risk of minor complications. Coronary stents open up arteries in the heart that are partially blocked by plaque, which reduces chest pain and improves the odds of surviving a heart attack. A C-section is an operation that removes a baby from its mother's uterus and is generally performed when normal delivery is not possible. C-sections have notably improved infant and mother mortality rates, although some people argue that C-sections are performed too often in the United States—where C-section rates are the highest in the world.

These technologies are now available to a wider range of people, which decreases mortality and increases lifespans, but also increases the cost of health care. Nevertheless, these costs are largely considered justifiable and, in the United States, access to advanced medical technology is assumed by most Americans to be a part of health care. Americans rely on medical technology not only to save and extend life, but also to provide a higher quality of life for people who are unwell. For example, reconstructive plastic surgery means people who have been burned or otherwise disfigured can have their bodies fixed and return to a normal lifestyle. Artificial cardiac pacemakers make it possible for those with heart irregularities to function normally and live longer. Assistive and adaptive technologies help people with disabilities interact with and move through the world, and for some, to maintain an independent lifestyle.

Some medical professionals belive that technology is overused in the health-care field. In a 2005 *Virtual Mentor* article, Dr. Carl Elliott argues, "The quality of life in question is not necessarily that of people who are sick. A growing number of medical technologies are employed to improve the looks, performance, and psychological well-being of people who are healthy."

When it comes to end-of-life care, medical technology may not always boost quality of life. Some doctors argue that performing tests on patients whom they know will die soon and subjecting them to treatments that may prolong life is unethical. Dr. Kenneth Fisher, quoted in a 2008 article by Linda S. Mah of the *Kalamazoo Gazette*, implores individuals, caregivers, doctors, nurses, and policy makers to reconsider expensive medical interventions at the end of life and focus instead on hospice and palliative care. Fisher cites a 1996 study that found end-of-life costs jumped to astronomical heights in the final year of life. While medical expenses for people over the age of sixty-five averaged $7,365 per year, in the last year of life expenses rose to $37,581—a 20 percent increase. Fisher describes this situation as "a moral tragedy."

How people use medical technology determines its value to society, and every person brings a different perspective and set of values to the doctor's office or emergency room. Quality of life is just one aspect of how medical technology affects the health-care industry. *Opposing Viewpoints: Medical Technology* examines the ways in which medical technology benefits and hinders society in the following chapters: "Does Medical Technology Provide Better Patient Outcomes?," "How Does Medical Technology Affect Health-Care Costs?," "How Do Electronic Medical Records Impact Patients?," and "What Is the Government's Role in Medical Technology?"

CHAPTER 1

Does Medical Technology Provide Better Patient Outcomes?

Chapter Preface

Patients in the United States pay a lot of money for health care annually—approximately $2.6 trillion in 2010, according to the Kaiser Family Foundation's 2012 report—and expect that they will receive the latest, most technically advanced treatments. But the latest treatments may not always be the best solution to a patient's problem. Researchers and policy makers argue that further studies must be done to determine the efficacy of new medical technology.

For example, electronic prescriptions are becoming common in the United States, paralleling the government-sponsored push to digitize all medical records by 2015. A study by Rainu Kaushal et al., published in the *Journal of General Internal Medicine* in 2010, showed a reduction in prescription errors for physicians who switched from paper-based prescriptions to electronic prescriptions—from 42.5 errors per 100 prescriptions to 6.6 per 100.

Despite such compelling evidence of making patient care more safe and efficient, the cost of implementing an electronic prescription system is considered high—prohibitively so for some practices. A 2007 study by the US Department of Health and Human Services (HHS), "How Much Does an E-prescribing System Cost?," pegged installation of an e-prescription system for ten full-time doctors at a psychiatric clinic at $40,000 with a $14,000 annual maintenance cost. HHS generalizes the cost of e-prescribing systems at $2,500 per physician.

The think tank RAND Health published a 2005 report, "Research Highlights: Electronic Prescribing Systems," expressing early concerns for the unintended errors that e-prescriptions can introduce, such as doctors and pharmacists assuming the system is correct and not checking their work, inappropriate dosing for different conditions, and ignoring system alerts. Despite RAND's concerns, the think tank also proposed that these problems should not be a barrier to implementation and would be overcome with further research and development.

Electronic prescription systems are the wave of the future in medical technology. In the following chapter, authors debate how medical technology such as electronic prescription systems helps or harms the health-care industry.

> *"In countless ways, medical technologies can improve access to care, improve the effectiveness of care, decrease morbidity and mortality, speed up recovery, and increase patient comfort."*

Improved Medical Technology Leads to Better Overall Health

Nadeem Esmail and Dominika Wrona

In the following viewpoint, two researchers argue that advances in medical technology have improved patient care. The authors examine studies that illuminate the improved mortality, shorter hospital stays, and better physician care of those who utilize newer technologies. They conclude that the increasing price of new technology is worthwhile because the increased life expectancy of those who benefit improves society. Nadeem Esmail is the director of the Centre for Health System Performance Studies and manager of the Alberta Policy Research Centre at the Fraser Institute. Dominika Wrona is a Fraser Institute intern and MBA student at the University of Toronto.

As you read, consider the following questions:

1. According to the authors, what is the quantifiable improvement Molyneux et al. found in patients treated

Nadeem Esmail and Dominika Wrona, "The Benefits of Medical Technologies," *Medical Technology in Canada*, August 2008, pp. 5–13. Copyright © 2008 by the Fraser Institute. All rights reserved. Reproduced by permission.

with neurosurgical clipping versus endovascular coil embolization?

2. What factors did Wang and Jamison determine led to better health outcomes in different countries, as detailed in the viewpoint?

3. According to the authors, what was the improved life expectancy of heart attack patients from 1984 to 1998?

Advanced medical technologies can deliver numerous benefits to both patients and those funding the health care system. According to Australia's Productivity Commission, medical technologies "... have reduced disease risk factors, long-term complications of related chronic diseases, and the need for drugs. They have also improved mobility and day-to-day functioning, and reduced hospital admissions, length of stay, and the indirect costs of caring for patient." Further, significant advances in the field of diagnostic equipment, surgical and laboratory procedures, and non-surgical equipment have increased hospital efficiency as well as patient comfort and safety. New medical devices and interventions are also able to offer patients treatments and diagnoses previously unavailable.

For example, newer advanced diagnostic equipment such as multi-slice Computed Tomography (CT) scanners, more powerful Magnetic Resonance Imaging (MRI) machines, and Positron Emission Tomography (PET) scanners (both stand-alone and combination PET/CT units) allow for greater accuracy, speed, and efficiency in diagnosing medical problems. They also provide less invasive procedures for the diagnosis of disease, which can facilitate earlier and more localized treatment. Doctors can use more sophisticated scanners to observe and learn more about the body's functions and location of disease without subjecting the patient to surgery for either diagnosis or needless interventions. For example, a PET scan

can detect a lung cancer that has spread, and thus avoid a fu-tile operation. It can also determine if liver tumours can be safely removed, and can help determine if chemotherapy treat-ment is working, or whether the drug cocktail being provided needs to be changed. PET scanners also allow some patients to avoid surgical biopsies for the diagnosis and identification of cancers.

Improved Surgical Technologies
Reduce Trauma and Hospital Stays

Due to innovation in surgical technologies, surgeons are now able to use specialized instruments to reduce the impact of treatment on patients. For example, surgeons today might use a video camera to enter the body through small incisions, and then move the camera lens and their surgical tools through tis-sue and blood vessels to the affected area, rather than opening the entire body cavity as was once common. Thanks to mini-mally invasive surgical techniques, procedures that once re-quired patients stay in hospital for days can now be performed on an outpatient basis. For example, surgical complications, time spent in hospital, and the amount of trauma to the patient have been significantly reduced by replacing conventional cho-lecystectomy (gall bladder removal) with minimally invasive laparoscopic cholecystectomy.

New laboratory procedures have also played an important role in identifying certain medical conditions, or predispositions to them. Armed with increased knowledge about the potential risks for developing certain conditions or diseases, patients have the impetus to be proactive about those diseases by altering their lifestyles and increasing their surveillance of the condition. For example, laboratory tests can determine mutations in the BRCA1 and BRCA2 genes, which can signal a higher risk of certain can-cers like breast cancer or ovarian cancer.

Advances in medical technology can also improve non-surgical hospital services. For example, electronic storage of diagnostic images can increase the efficiency of patient information transfer and ensure faster turnaround times. Electronically stored diagnostic images can also allow for long-distance contracting by reducing or eliminating the need to physically handle and transport images. As another example, automated medication dispensing systems can decrease the incidence of medical errors in drug distribution and can reduce the time pharmacists and nurses spend on drug dispensing.

New medical devices can also offer new treatment options to patients who were previously left untreated. Consider the Implantable Cardioverter Defibrillator (ICD), which works on the same principal as an external defibrillator, but is implanted in a patient's chest. The ICD sends an electrical current to the heart when it detects serious arrhythmia, or a stoppage, in order to restore normal rhythm. This device allows patients at risk of sudden cardiac arrest to live independently and not be under constant surveillance.

Studies Show a Decline in Heart Patient Mortality

In countless ways, medical technologies can improve access to care, improve the effectiveness of care, decrease morbidity and mortality, speed up recovery, and increase patient comfort. These benefits are not just theoretical, but have been quantified in published studies.

[Dr. M.G. Myriam] Hunink et al. studied the decline in mortality rates due to coronary heart disease between 1980 and 1990. The authors estimated that 25 percent of the decline could be explained by primary prevention (reduction of coronary heart disease incidence), and 43 percent could be explained by improvements in the treatment of patients with coronary heart disease. That is, improvements in patient treatment between 1980 and 1990 explained almost half of the decline in mortality from coronary heart disease. Eugene Braunwald, a renowned cardiologist and researcher, stated:

Diagnostic imaging of the heart, great vessels, and coronary arteries . . . has greatly facilitated cardiac diagnosis. Notable therapeutic advances include the development of open-heart surgery for the treatment of many forms of congenital and acquired heart disease; catheter-based interventions, such as coronary angioplasty and stenting, for the nonsurgical treatment of coronary artery disease; and cardiac pacemakers and implanted cardiac defibrillators for a variety of life threatening cardiac arrhythmias. These procedures . . . have improved the quality and, increasingly, the duration of life. Braunwald goes on to say that advances in cardiac imaging "will facilitate the early identification of patients at high risk for serious coronary events." He adds that "newly developing catheter-based techniques for coronary revascularization that incorporate new approaches to prevent restenosis [i.e., the closing of an artery that was previously opened by a cardiac procedure] should help to reduce the incidence of acute coronary events." . . .

Advancing Medical Technology Improves Neurosurgical Outcomes

[S.C.] Johnston et al. compared the outcomes of treating unruptured cerebral aneurysms with the common procedure of surgical clipping (performed by neurosurgeons) and the newer, less invasive alternative of endovascular coil embolization (performed by neurointerventional radiologists). The authors found that surgery was associated with greater rates of new disability, an increased likelihood of reporting new symptoms or disability after treatment, more complications, and longer recovery. Surgical patients also experienced longer hospital stays (7.7 days, on average, for surgery compared with 5.0 days for embolization) and higher hospital charges ($38,000, on average, for surgery compared with $33,400 for embolization).

Similarly, [D.H.] Molyneux et al. compared outcomes of treating ruptured intracranial aneurysms with neurosurgical clipping and endovascular coiling in 2,143 patients. The study found that 23.5 percent of patients treated with endovascular coiling were dead or dependent one year after treatment (8.0 percent dead, 2.6 percent fully dependent, 2.8 percent partially dependent, and 10.1 percent with significant restriction in lifestyle) compared to 30.9 percent of patients treated with neurosurgery (9.9 percent, 3.6 percent, 4.0 percent, and 13.4 percent respectively). This difference in survival was statistically significant and persisted for at least 7 years after treatment. The study also found that the risk of epilepsy was substantially lower in patients who received endovascular treatment. Conversely, though the risk of late rebleeding was still low, it was higher than for those treated with neurosurgery.

Medical Innovation Improves Mortality Rates

Frank R. Lichtenberg measured the effect of innovation in five areas of medical procedures and products: pathology and laboratory procedures, outpatient prescription drugs, inpatient prescription drugs, surgical procedures, and diagnostic radiology procedures, on the mortality and disability of Americans who were afflicted with a condition whose treatment was affected by innovation between 1990 and 2003. The study found positive and significant correlations between lab innovation and outpatient drug innovation, and mortality. The study also found that conditions with higher rates of laboratory and outpatient drug innovation exhibited greater increases in the mean age at death. Lichtenberg estimated the increase in the mean age at death resulting from the use of new laboratory procedures to be approximately 6 months, or 42 percent of the total increase (1.18 years), in the mean age at death observed over the period in the sample of diseases. He further estimated that new laboratory procedures introduced between 1990 and 1998 had saved 1.13 million life-years in 1998 (2.31 million people who died in 1998 multiplied by the extra 6 months they lived due to new laboratory procedures).

Summary of Research on the Value of Medical Technology Changes

Condition	Years	Change in treatment costs	Outcome		
			Change	Value	Net benefit
Heart attack	1984–98	$10,000	One-year increase in life expectancy	$70,000	$60,000
Low-birthweight infants	1950–90	$40,000	Twelve-year increase in life expectancy	$240,000	$200,000
Depression	1991–96	$0	Higher remission probability at some cost for those already treated		
		<$0	More people treated, with benefits exceeding costs.		
Cataracts	1969–98	$0	Substantial improvements in quality at no cost increase for those already treated		
		<$0	More people treated, with benefits exceeding costs		
Breast cancer	1985–96	$20,000	Four-month increase in life expectancy	$20,000	$0

TAKEN FROM: Nadeem Esmail and Dominika Wrona, "Medical Technology in Canada," *Studies in Health Care Policy*, Fraser Institute, August 2008.

Potential Annual Savings If Existing Surgical Procedures for Eight Diseases Were Replaced with Interventional Radiology Procedures, in Appropriate Circumstances

Disease	Treatment savings ($ millions)	Societal savings ($ millions)	No. of hospital bed-days saved	No. of patient lives saved
Peripheral arterial disease (iliac)	21.0	1.1	6,497	34
Peripheral arterial disease (lower extremity)	26.6	2.5	14,691	54
Abdominal aortic aneurysm	-5.0	8.5	6,559	43
Ischemic stroke	-1.1	0.4	2,439	23
Cerebral aneurysm	15.2	0.8	4,834	67
Uterine fibroids	38.5	78.3	58,768	34
Vertebral fracture (vertebroplasty)	59.7	ND	ND	0
Liver cancer	25.4	0.7	4,222	147
Total	180.3	> 92.3	98,010	402

ND = not determined.

TAKEN FROM: Nadeem Esmail and Dominika Wrona, "Medical Technology in Canada," *Studies in Health Care Policy*, Fraser Institute, August 2008.

Medical Technology Advances Lead to Shorter Hospital Stays

A recent [2007] report by the Canadian Institute for Health Information looked at trends in hospital use. It suggested that "advances in medical technology [are] leading to more efficient ways of treating inpatient." The report also found that more operations are being performed as outpatient day surgeries across Canada; the number of hospital procedures performed as outpatient day surgeries increased by 30.6 percent over 10 years, while the number of inpatient surgeries decreased by 16.5 percent. The total number of surgeries increased by 17.3 percent. Further, the age-standardized hospitalization rate decreased by 25 percent over the 10 years, falling from roughly 11 out of 100 Canadians being hospitalized in 1995–1996, to roughly 8 out of every 100 Canadians in 2005–2006. The total number of days Canadians spent in acute care hospitals had also decreased, falling from approximately 23 million days in 1995–1996 to 20 million in 2006 (a 13.1 percent reduction). Moreover, even though the average length of hospital stay remained unchanged since 1995–1996 at 7.2 days, the age-adjusted national average length of hospital stay decreased from 7.5 days in 1995–1996 to 7 days in 2005–2006 (a 6.7 percent decrease). The report made no explicit link between the reduced length of hospital stay, the reduced likelihood of hospitalization, the increased reliance on outpatient day surgery, and advances in medical technology. However, the correlation between advances in medical technology (pharmaceutical, surgical, diagnostic, and otherwise) and shorter hospital stays is worth noting and has been confirmed by studies examining some forms of medical technologies. . . .

Medical Technology Improves Physician Care

[J.] Wang and [D.] Jamison, in a study examining differences in mortality across OECD nations, found that the "availability of medical technology appears to play a significant role in improving the efficiency of health care provided by doctors (to reduce mortality) across countries." More specifically, they found after controlling for factors such as income and the number of physicians, that countries with a higher long-term availability of MRI and CT scanners (used as proxies for technology generally) produce better health outcomes in terms of life expectancy and potential years of life lost to heart disease. In other words, this study suggests that there is an important beneficial relationship between the supply of medical technologies and the impact of physician care.

Advances in Medical Technology Are Worth the Cost

The studies examining the medical benefits of advances in technology discussed above show that advanced medical technologies can reduce mortality, increase longevity, and increase quality of life. However, these new technologies can be expensive and their costs are often cited as reasons for the lack of investment. A common concern is whether the benefits of medical technologies are worth their cost. Several studies address this issue directly.

In the paper measuring the effect of innovation in laboratory procedures discussed above, Frank R. Lichtenberg determined the cost per life-year gained from the new laboratory procedures was estimated to be $6,093. According to Lichtenberg, this value is generally considered to be "quite cost-effective." Similarly, [Dale A.] Rublee, in a review of access to medical technology, states that computerized diagnosis and lithotripsy can be both quality enhancing and cost saving.

[David M.] Cutler and [Mark B.] McClellan reported on a series of studies showing the disease-level costs and benefits of medical advances in five conditions: heart attacks, low birth weight, depression, cataracts, and breast cancer. The study primarily measured increased longevity and increased productivity of patients as a result of the introduction of medical technology. Cutler and McClellan concluded that even though technological change has accounted for a significant portion of medical care cost increases over time, medical spending as a whole is worth the cost. . . .

For example, according to the study, life expectancy for the average person following a heart attack was just short of 5 years in 1984, but by 1998 it had risen to 6 years. Assuming the additional year of life was valued at $100,000 and the annual cost of living was estimated to be $25,000 during that additional year of life, Cutler and McClellan estimated the benefit to society of an additional year of life for heart attack patients to be $75,000. Including an accounting for the time-value of money (a dollar given six years from now is worth less to an individual today than is a dollar given today), the present value of the benefits from technological change was found to be $70,000. Since the treatment costs increased by $10,000 between 1984 and 1998 as a result of technological innovation that both replaced older forms of care and provided existing technologies to more patients, the net benefit from new technology was estimated to be approximately $60,000.

The Cost Outweighs the Benefit

Cutler and McClellan (2001) also reviewed studies examining the costs and benefits of technological change in the treatment of low birth weight infants, depression, cataracts, and breast cancer. They found that the estimated benefit of technological change in all but the latter was much greater than the cost. Though outcomes were improved by advances in the treatment of breast cancer, the increase in costs was roughly equal to the societal benefit, which led to the conclusion that, in this instance, "technological change was neither beneficial nor harmful on net."

The study concluded that the cost of technology for heart attacks, low birth weight, depression and cataracts is high, but it is outweighed by the value of health benefits that accrued from the introduction and use of these technologies. Although only 5 conditions were analyzed in the study, the results have implications for the health care system more broadly. The report states: "The benefits from lower infant mortality and better treatment of heart attacks have been sufficiently great that they alone are about equal to the entire cost increase for medical care over time. Thus, recognizing that there are other benefits to medical care, we conclude that medical spending as a whole is clearly worth the cost."

A study by Cutler finds that revascularization, or re-establishing adequate blood supply, following a heart attack (including angioplasty and coronary artery bypass grafting) is also a cost-effective technological innovation. Specifically, the study examines the survival and care costs for US Medicare patients over a 17-year period following their heart attacks. Cutler determines that revascularization results in a 1.1 year increase in life expectancy at a cost of approximately $38,000 ($33,246 per year of life gained) if the benefits of revascularization flow directly from the treatment, or a 0.08 year increase in life expectancy at a cost of approximately $1,389 ($17,022 per year of life gained) if admission to a hospital with revascularization capabilities is the source of benefits for patients. Either way, Cutler finds that the care provided is clearly worth the cost, whether the care provided is revascularization itself, or the quality of care provided by hospitals with revascularization capabilities.

Minimally Invasive Procedures Save Money

A study commissioned by the Canadian Association of Radiologists and the Canadian Interventional Radiology Association showed that significant savings could be realized if existing surgical procedures were replaced with interventional radiology (minimally invasive procedures performed using image guidance). Specifically, the study found that for 8 diseases, replacing existing surgical procedures with interventional radiology procedures in appropriate circumstances could potentially save

402 Canadian lives annually, as well as 98,010 hospital bed-days, $180.3 million in direct treatment costs, and more than $92.3 million in societal costs. . . . (These costs include indirect health care savings associated with faster recovery and return to work, and less follow-up visits.) These savings calculations were not net-of-costs; the study estimated that an annual budget of $221.3 million would be required to realize the annual savings. . . .

The evidence reviewed above finds that medical technologies can increase longevity, reduce mortality, and improve quality of life for those fortunate enough to have access to them. Medical technologies can often accomplish these improvements cost effectively, and in some cases can reduce costs while improving outcomes. Thus, a high quality health care program should provide individuals with a high level of access to medical technologies; not doing so would be to the detriment of patients. Does Canada's health care program live up to the claim that it is a high quality program?

| *"We are by far the most over-treated, over-medicalized people in the history of the world."*

Improved Medical Technology Does Not Lead to Better Overall Health

Sharyn Alfonsi and Courtney Hutchison

In the following viewpoint, two journalists discuss a Centers for Disease Control and Prevention (CDC) report that shows a sharp increase in the use of advanced medical technology in the United States. The authors maintain that research data does not support a direct link between longer life and new medical technology. They cite experts who claim that, while medical technology has its benefits, more needs to be done to rein in unnecessary testing. Sharyn Alfonsi is an ABC News correspondent; Courtney Hutchison is a senior associate at Global Health Strategies and a former ABC News reporter.

As you read, consider the following questions:

1. According to the authors, approximately how many Americans were taking three or more prescriptions in 1994?

2. How much has the use of statin drugs increased from the early 1990s to 2006, according to the authors?

3. How were medical problems diagnosed in the 1960s, according to Dr. Daniel Kopans?

M ore drugs, more tests, more surgery.

A report by the U.S. Centers for Disease Control and Prevention [CDC] shows that the use of high-tech medical tests and surgeries has escalated rapidly over the past decade in the United States. But whether the expanding presence of medical technology is a good thing is still a matter of debate.

The rates of Americans getting MRIs [magnetic resonance imaging] and CT [computed tomography] scans tripled between 1996 and 2006, according to the report released today [February 17, 2010] from the National Center for Health Statistics. CT scans can help doctors detect everything from kidney stones to cancer, but they pack a mega dose of radiation— as much as 500 times that of a conventional X-ray, which some health experts say raises the risk for cancer.

More Americans are also going under the knife. According to the report, the rate of knee replacement procedures increased 70 percent over the decade studied; kidney and liver transplants increased by 31 percent and 43 percent, respectively.

What's more, Americans are also on more drugs now than in years past: 47 percent of the population in 2006 was taking at least one prescription drug, compared to 38 percent in 1994. About one in five Americans in 2006 were taking three or more prescriptions—nearly double that in 1994.

Of course, increased use of new medical technology and a spike in the use of prescription drugs has occurred alongside a continual increase in life expectancy and decrease in death rates for cancer, heart disease, and stroke. The connection between these two trends remains unclear, however, experts say.

Advanced Medical Technology Can Reduce Quality of Care

Physicians sometimes request unnecessary tests or treatments in order to avoid medico-legal liability for a missed diagnosis or treatment opportunity. In other situations, having a low tolerance for ambiguity by doctor or patient similarly may lead to unnecessary investigation and treatment. The analysis suggests that defensive medicine is not merely a problem of increased cost, but also one of reduced quality-of-care.

Newer diagnostic technologies are able to detect ever smaller or milder abnormalities that aggravate the problem. Many of the small abnormalities detected with new imaging techniques are often clinically irrelevant. Spinal MRI exemplifies the problem of discovering more and more abnormalities with most having no clinical relevance. An Institute of Medicine study concluded that lumbar spine surgery is overused and misused in United States, and the wide use of imaging studies may be a driver of this excess use.

L.T.H. Tan and K.L. Ong, "The Impact
of Medical Technology on Healthcare Today,"
Hong Kong Journal of Emergency Medicine,
vol. 9, no. 4, October 2002, pp. 231–236.

Medical Technology Does Not Lead to Longer Life Expectancy

Still, considering the overall rise in life expectancy, some doctors say Americans are more healthy for the increase in medical interventions.

"Death rates are down for things like heart disease and stroke, which I would suspect has to do with better diagnosis [through diagnostic imaging technology] and people going on preventive medications like statins," says Dr. Daniel Kopans, director of the Breast Imaging Division at Massachusetts General Hospital. The CDC found a ten-fold increase in the use of statin [cholesterol lowering] drugs from 1988–1994 to 2003–2006.

But according to Dr. Nortin Hadler, professor of Medicine and Microbiology/Immunology at the University of North Carolina at Chapel Hill and author of *Worried Sick* and *The Last Well Person*, "We may be fooling ourselves as a society" in thinking that all this technology is actually making us live longer.

"The decrease in premature death can be traced back long before we had many important interventions," Hadler says. "[It is] not clear that all of our high-tech knowledge is responsible for this. . . . The data is consistent that if we never perform a single stent or angioplasty, we would not change the happy outcome of fewer people having and/or dying from heart attacks."

Still, he says, most in the public assume that the high-tech interventions are responsible, which drives up demand.

"Our society has learned that we are technologically dependent for our longevity. So you put together this notion that without all the high-tech we would all be in big trouble and the fact that advantaged areas of society are living longer and you have a perfect marketing storm," he says.

"We are by far the most over-treated, over-medicalized people in the history of the world," he says.

Does Advanced Technology Improve Health Care?

That Americans are over-treated has become a common claim in light of sky-rocketing health-care costs, but diagnostic experts dispute Hadler's argument that our advanced technology is not actually improving health care.

"I know what healthcare was like in the '60s and '70s," says Dr. Herb Kressel, radiologist-in-chief at Beth Israel Deaconess Medical Center in Boston. "There's no doubt in my mind that we're doing a better job . . . no doubt that in part [the decrease in mortality] is due to technology. The problem is how we use the resources effectively to prolong life and improve quality of life."

Kopans cites unexplained abdominal pain as an example: In the 1960s, exploratory surgery often would be used to diagnose the problem—a painful and somewhat risky process that today is done easily and painlessly with CT scans and ultrasound. And he says that technological advances have had similar benefits for breast biopsies; whereas invasive surgery was once needed, now ultrasounds allow the biopsy to be done with needles.

Both Kopans and Kressel agree that overuse of these technologies—especially diagnostic or screening tests—is a problem. But they say it is not one that should be solved by using less technology across the board, but rather by using technology selectively, where it is needed, and where it can do the most good.

A substantial part of over-utilization of this technology is "reflecting defensive medicine," Kressel says, where doctors fear that if they don't provide every test, than they will be liable when they miss a diagnosis.

"The trick is we really need research to know how to use these tools in a manner that will be preventive and predictive, to tailor the tests and interventions to what the patient really needs," Kressel says.

And this may be where the two sides meet. Hadler says that when this new technology is used for a specific diagnostic purpose, that is likely to provide insight into healing.

"Now that's a medical advance," Hadler says.

> *"With robot control and assistance, surgery for any kind of injury or ailment is faster, more accurate, and less invasive than ever before."*

Minimally Invasive Robotic Surgery Shortens Recovery and Reduces Risks

Roger Allan

In the following viewpoint, an electronics journalist examines the growing field of robot-assisted surgery. According to the author, the development of robots for surgery has led to a laparoscopic gripping hand; thin, flexible tools that can snake through the body with small or no incisions; and robots that are MRI-compatible. He acknowledges that cost is a restrictive factor in adopting robots in surgery, but contends that the benefits are too important to not continue research and adoption of robotic surgical tools. Roger Allan is a leading journalist in the field of electronics and served as executive editor of Electronic Design *for fifteen years.*

As you read, consider the following questions:

1. According to Allan, what are the three surgical categories of medical robot systems?

2. What are the benefits, as argued by the author, to robot assistance in knee replacement surgery?
3. What is the Imperial College of London's $4.2 million project, as described by Allan?

Advances in robotics technology are completely transforming today's hospital operating rooms. With robot control and assistance, surgery for any kind of injury or ailment is faster, more accurate, and less invasive than ever before. Because robots help accelerate procedures, operations become safer. With conventional surgery, a surgeon performing an operation lasting several hours can become exhausted. As a result, the surgeon's hand can be subject to harmful errors, particularly for complicated and delicate tasks like neurosurgeries. But a robot hand never tires, and it won't waver out of position.

Improvements in sensing (particularly haptic sensing), imaging, better robotic control and articulation, and the development of robots that are more dexterous have spurred the dramatic rise in robotic surgery. The medical community is now developing a greater understanding of its benefits as well as the processes involved in ensuring seamless interfacing between a surgeon and a robotic system.

The Role of Medical Robots

Medical robots aren't completely autonomous, and they don't perform the surgery by themselves. Instead, they assist the surgeon, who commands and controls them. As a result, surgery is fast becoming a partnership between man and machine. According to BCC Research, the market for surgical robots in the U.S. alone will total $2.5 billion by 2011. This market is projected to grow between 2006 and 2011 by an expected annual growth rate of 43%.

Medical robots are assisting in urological, neurological, gynecological, cardiac, orthopedic, gastrointestinal, pediatric, and radio-surgical procedures. Depending on the degree of the surgeon's interaction during an operation, these systems can be broadly divided into three categories: supervisory-controlled, telesurgical, and shared-control systems.

During supervisor-controlled surgeries, the robot executes the procedure in response to programmed computer inputs from the surgeon. In telesurgery (or remote surgery), the surgeon manipulates the robot's hand from a distance using real-time imaging and haptic feedback. Surgeons are most involved in shared-control procedures, where they use the robot to obtain "steady hand" manipulation of the surgical instruments in use.

The U.S. government also is pursuing robotic surgery. The Trauma Pod program from the Defense Advanced Research Projects Agency (DARPA) envisions the operating room of the future. Led by SRI, this multiphased program seeks to use robotics to project the skills of surgeons to precisely where they're needed on the battlefield. It includes contributions from the universities of Washington, Texas, and Maryland; Oak Ridge National Laboratory; General Dynamics; Intuitive Surgical; General Electric; Integrated Medical Systems; and Robotic Surgical Tech.

The most notable product on the market, the da Vinci Surgical System from Intuitive Surgical Co., consists of a viewing and control console and a surgical arm unit. Used worldwide, it's the only robotic-assisted device being used for laproscopic as well as a variety of minimally invasive keyhole surgeries. It's also been used successfully in a number of gynecological, urological, and cardiac procedures.

The Future of Virtual Surgeries

For all its advantages, robotic surgery still needs better computer modeling, image processing, and haptic sensing for a more seamless integration of man and machine in surgical operations. Such improvements will enable better pre-surgical planning, too, allowing doctors to perform virtual surgeries before the actual operation.

The University of Washington is developing a "holomer" system that serves as a total body scan to guide intra-operative navigation during surgery. A surgeon can then use this information to perform a virtual operation on a patient prior to performing the real operation.

That's also the goal at the Johns Hopkins University Engineering Research Center for Computer Integrated Systems and Technology. Its surgical CAD-CAM system offers "one-stop shopping" to integrate re-planning through post-operation evaluation and to create modular systems for "plug-and-play" surgery.

Improving Robotic Sense of Touch

The researchers also are investigating the sense of touch, which is very important in delicate surgeries. "Surgeons have asked for this kind of feedback. So we're using our understanding of haptic technology to try to give surgeons back the sense of touch they lose when they use robotic medical tools," says Allison Okamura, a leading researcher in man-machine interaction at Johns Hopkins.

Sensors could be attached to the robotic tools to convey how much force is being applied to, say, a surgical suture. Also, mathematical models would represent the moves made by the robotic tools, and this data would be converted to haptic feedback sent to the surgeon.

Okamura's team developed a visual haptics system that sends haptic information observed by a surgeon on a display during suturing. A colored circle follows the image of the suturing tool, with red showing too much force (where a suture might snap) and green and yellow indicating just the right amount of suture force.

Researchers at Tufts University are also investigating methods of simulating minimally invasive surgery that uses visualization coupled with haptics to incorporate feedback into robotic surgical training. They're concentrating on developing tools for laproscopic surgery using a video camera and force-feedback sensors.

"In teleoperation, force feedback or haptic feedback is very important," says Caroline Cao, assistant professor of mechanical engineering at Tufts. "Otherwise, you don't feel what it is that you're dealing with. You end up either colliding into your targets or you don't know how to control the forces in order to manipulate your target."

The Importance of Vision Sensing

With vision-sensing platforms, surgical robots see where a procedure is being used as well as how precisely that procedure is being performed. These platforms are essential to bringing accurate and affordable robotic surgery to the market. One company, Prosurgics, is collaborating with Adept Technology to produce next-generation surgical robotic systems.

"This collaboration will combine our expertise in robotics for image-guided and navigated neurological and soft-tissue surgery with those of Adept Technology in robotic control and vision-guided applications to provide affordable surgical robotic products for improved patient care and optimized economies for healthcare providers," says Colin Robertson, Prosurgics' business development marketing director.

"Our experience in image-guided robotics is very broad and strong. This includes the assembly and manufacturing of mobile phones, computer disk drives, solar cells, and food handling. It will provide valuable assistance to the medical robotics field," adds Dave Pap Rocki, Adept Technology's chief technology officer.

Prosurgics offers advanced surgical tools like the PathFinder, an image-guided manipulator for precise localization in neurosurgical procedures. With this technology, surgeons can position stereotactic instruments to within an accuracy of 1 mm. The firm additionally makes the EndoAssist, an image-guided manipula-

Robotic Surgery Reduces Surgeon's Tremor

One of the advantages of the robotic surgery compared with the open or laparoscopic techniques is that it virtually eliminates the surgeon's tremor, which can be crucial when handling sensitive and delicate structures such as the nerves, blood vessels and sphincters.

"Clinical: Improving Outcomes with Surgical Precision," GP, *April 10, 2009, p. 40.*

tor for endoscopes that's used in minimally invasive thoracic and abdominal surgeries.

The Growth of Robotic Orthopedics

Image-guided orthopedic robotic surgeries represent one of the fastest growing medical areas. Approximately 400,000 people each year have knee-replacement surgery, which generally requires lengthy surgical incisions and can cause a considerable amount of pain. Moreover, patients face lengthy recovery times before they're on their feet. This is changing, though, with robotic orthopedic procedures that require shorter incisions, are less painful, and allow for much faster recovery times.

A study involving engineers and surgeons from the Imperial College of London shows that robotic assistance improves accuracy in knee surgery, leading to knee replacements that function better and last longer than conventional surgical techniques. The study was funded by the Acrobot Co. Ltd., a spin-out of the Imperial College of London.

One prominent procedure is MAKOplasty knee resurfacing from Mako Surgical Corp. Its tactile guidance system (TGS) allows surgeons to accurately plan the size of the knee implant and optimize the implant's position and orientation, relative to a CT scan taken before surgery.

The Robodoc surgical assistant system from Integrated Surgical Systems also supports image-guided orthopedic surgery. It integrates the company's Orthodoc Presurgical Planner with a computer-controlled robot for jointreplacement surgeries. It can also be used for neurosurgical procedures.

The German Federal Ministry of Education and Research is funding orthoMIT, a "Gentle Surgery by Innovative Technology" project known as SOMIT. It aims to develop an intelligent platform for gentle operative therapy in robotic orthopedic and traumatology procedures, particularly hip, knee, and spinal-column surgery.

Robotic radiosurgery has also been shown as an excellent alternative treatment for tumors. The Cyber Knife from Accuray and the Gamma Knife from Elekta use highly precise beams of radiation to destroy tumors quickly, painlessly, and without downtime or lengthy hospital stays. Tumors anywhere in the body can be treated, even those previously considered untreatable. Using CT images, these tools enable surgeons to construct a very precise pre-surgical plan to deliver a total dose of radiation to the tumor while minimally exposing the surrounding normal tissues.

The Future of Robotic Technology

Minimally invasive "keyhole-like" robotic surgeries will continue to make strides with even greater agility. The payoff will be shorter patient hospital stays, more accurate and effective procedures, and lower risks (e.g., infections) thanks to smaller surgical openings and faster procedures. For example, Japan's Tokyo Institute of Technology is investigating an approach that allows the assembly of robotic components within the body, prior to surgery, to assist in robotic surgeries on large and slippery internal organs like the liver.

These researchers are developing a three-fingered steel hand, with each finger 5 cm long, for grasping internal organs. They're using a hollow arm, 30 cm long and 16 mm in diameter, that's inserted into the body via a small incision. The three fingers are then passed part of the way through a nearby keyhole and then snapped into place on the arm. Stiff wires along the arm allow the fingers to grasp organs. Experiments inside a dummy body cavity have shown this approach to be effective.

At Johns Hopkins University, researchers hope to soon unveil advanced robotic grippers and retractors with force sensors for human trial runs. These tools will allow surgeons to avoid gripping blood vessels too tightly. Additionally, they will allow oxygen sensors to differentiate diseased tissue from healthy tissue. One tool flexes much like an elephant trunk to glide down a patient's throat for scar-less repairs of the upper airways. Another tool that's now under development will let surgeons bust eye clots inside minuscule blood vessels.

Robotic snake-like tools are under development at the Imperial College of London and Carnegie Mellon University. The Imperial College's i-Snake project, a $4.2 million program funded by the Wellcome Trust, a large U.K. charity that funds innovative biomedical research, centers on a flexible robotic arm that acts as a surgeon's hands and eyes. The technology will permit surgeons to navigate difficult and restrictive regions of the body, such as the alimentary tract and cardiovascular pathways, faster and more precisely than they could while using conventional techniques.

Carnegie Mellon's miniature HeartLander facilitates minimally invasive therapy on the surface of the beating heart. Under physician control, the robot enters the chest through an incision below the sternum and adheres to the epicardial surface of the heart. It then autonomously navigates to the specified location and administers the treatment. Compared with existing approaches, it improves the precision and stability of interaction with the heart's surface while decreasing the morbidity associated with access.

One of the greatest challenges lies in developing a robotic system that works in a magnetic-resonance imaging (MRI) environment where surgery is being performed. MRIs have strong and sensitive magnetic fields that must be bypassed. Otherwise, the MRI image will be distorted. The Johns Hopkins PneuStep, a robotic tool that's designed for prostate surgery, alleviates these MRI problems.

PneuStep consists of six motors that power an MRI-compatible robot. Three pistons are connected to a series of gears. The gears are turned by air flow, which is in turn controlled by a computer located in a room adjacent to the MRI machine. The system can achieve precise and smooth motion up to 50 μm, finer than a human hair and well above that of a human surgeon. PneuStep is currently undergoing preclinical trials.

The neuroArm is another MRI-compatible robotic tool being developed at Canada's University of Calgary. This machine can provide precision motions up to 25 μm. It uses lead-zirconium-titanate (PZT) motors to move a small ceramic finger back and forth. The finger rotates a ceramic ring, creating motion through friction.

In the near term, cost will limit the widespread adoption of full-fledged large robotic surgical systems, which can go for $1 million or more and are expensive to maintain. Yet studies reveal that most surgeons who used such systems have become converts to this technology. Clearly, lower-cost systems are needed, and many researchers worldwide are busy working to reach that goal.

VIEWPOINT 4

"Some doctors argue that without much
authoritative research, the da Vinci
robot is more a marketing tool than an
improvement to surgery."

Robotic Surgery Offers Patients No Benefits over Traditional Surgery

Lisa Weidenfeld and Joseph Uchill

In the following viewpoint, two journalists maintain that the benefits of robotic surgical aids are slim or nonexistent over less expensive laparoscopic operations. While marketing and consumer expectation push the adoption of robotic surgical aids, the authors claim many doctors are still waiting for controlled studies to prove efficacy. Lisa Weidenfeld is a technology reporter for Medill News Service. Joseph Uchill graduated with a master's degree in journalism from Northwestern University in 2012.

As you read, consider the following questions:

1. According to Weidenfeld and Uchill, how much does a da Vinci surgical robot cost?

2. What is one of the most common operations that the da Vinci robot is used for, as described by the authors?
3. Instead of randomized trials, what is the method the authors say is used to study the efficacy of the da Vinci robot?

The new da Vinci surgical robot is a hit with patients, who request it for all kinds of procedures. But is it really more effective than traditional surgery—or just more expensive? Some doctors argue that without much authoritative research, the da Vinci robot is more a marketing tool than an improvement to surgery.

Surgeries performed with the new, high-tech, da Vinci robot use a narrower blade and provide greater precision than traditional open surgeries, which are performed with a scalpel. The machines are maneuvered by a surgeon operating the robotic arms from behind a nearby console.

There are 2,132 da Vinci systems world-wide, said Chris Simmonds, senior director of marketing services for manufacturer Intuitive Surgical, Inc. and that number is growing. But they do not come cheap. The machines each cost between $1.1 million and $2 million, with an additional cost of $100 thousand to $180 thousand for maintenance annually.

The "Glamor" of New Technology

In a 2011 study from Johns Hopkins University about the marketing of the da Vinci robot, 41 percent of hospital websites included a description of robotic surgery, with 89 percent of those descriptions claiming clinical superiority. Despite this claim, only 2 percent of those hospitals made a specific comparison to open or laparoscopic surgery, which involves inserting a camera through an incision. The marketing for robotic surgery may win over more converts than the results of the surgeries.

"You start to see this is not just a trivial issue of exuberant marketing, but it is in some cases potentially inaccurate and really harmful, potentially harmful information, wrapped in the glitz and the glamor of a new technology," said Gary Schwitzer, publisher of HealthNewsReview.org, a site devoted to reviewing media coverage of "medical treatments, tests, products and procedures." Schwitzer has been reporting on health issues for more than 30 years.

He said he first noticed heavy positive media coverage of robotics about three years ago and HealthNewsReview.org has since examined a number of articles about robotic surgery. The site often highlights the lack of critical analysis done by journalists. For example, in a May 2009 post, Schwitzer noted that a *Good Morning America* episode devoted to robotic surgery did not mention risks, the cost of the technology or treatment, independent research to verify results or other treatment options.

Robotic Surgery Has a Marginal Advantage

Dr. Enrico Benedetti, head of the department of surgery at University of Illinois Hospital Health and Sciences System called the robot a "tremendous advantage" but said it was a "cosmetic advantage more than anything." His group recently performed the first single port robotic gallbladder removal in the Midwest.

Single port surgery involves making only one incision to reduce scarring. The robotic method gives the surgeon a greater range of motion and increased visibility.

One of the most common uses of the robot is in prostate removal. The prostate cancer support group Us Too estimates every five minutes, two men are diagnosed with prostate cancer. Of that group, a 2010 *New York Times* article estimated that 86 percent of the ones who opted for surgery chose to have robot-assisted operations.

Yet despite the procedure's popularity, a 2008 study of Medicare patients found that adverse effects like sexual dysfunction and incontinence were no less frequent than with open surgery.

Prostate cancer survivor Bob Wright, an Us Too volunteer, chose to go through with a robotic procedure after talking to a coworker who had gone through it and recommended an experienced surgeon in San Antonio. Wright highlighted the benefits—a shorter hospital stay and decreased blood loss, as well as the increased range of motion provided by the robot that's not possible with laparoscopic surgery.

But Schwitzer said greater precision and control were not as important as the long-term results.

"If that doesn't translate to improved outcomes, then healthcare consumers should be asking, 'well, what do I care about greater precision and control?'"

Simmonds disagreed.

"We do think the surgery is proven," Simmonds said, pointing out that there have been more than 4,600 peer-reviewed papers published on da Vinci surgery.

Doctors Demand Controlled Studies

Another naysayer of robotic surgery writes a blog called *Skeptical Scalpel*. The anonymous blogger claims to have been a surgeon for 40 years and a surgical department chairman and residency program director for more than 23 of those years. *Skeptical Scalpel* publishes an extensive list of studies regarding the effectiveness of robotic surgery.

One 2009 study from the Royal Free Hospital and University College School of Medicine in London claims that robot-assisted gallbladder removal had no significant advantages over traditional laparoscopic ones.

Another report from the Department of Surgery at the Second Hospital of Lanzhou University in China in 2010 reviewed studies of robot-assisted surgery for acid reflux. It concluded that robotic surgery was a "feasible alternative" but that it lacked obvious advantages for extensive clinical application.

The standard of proof in medical research is the control study, which randomly determines the patients who get each treat-

Robotic Surgery Is Not a Panacea

"If you summarize all the literature we've got to date, it basically shows that for the long-term outcomes of curing cancer and recovering sexual and urinary function, the robotic surgery is either comparable to or not as good as open surgery," explains [Peter Scardino, M.D., a urologist at New York's Memorial Sloan-Kettering Cancer Center].

Lisa Farino, "Robotic Surgery for Prostate Cancer: An Automatic Choice?," MSN Health, February 23, 2011. health.msn.com.

ment, keeping that information secret even from the patients. Robotic surgery lacks the control studies that would comfort doctors such as Dr. Richard Hodin, chief of endocrine surgery at Massachusetts General Hospital in Boston.

Hodin said that "the number of good trials comparing robotic surgery are slim, if any."

Trials of the da Vinci Robot

"There have been 25 randomized trials carried out on da Vinci out of the 5,600," Simmonds said. "There have been attempts to do randomized trials over the years against open, but patients have not been willing to go into the open arm when given a choice."

Dr. Gerald Chodak, a urologist and prostate disease specialist, agreed that the likelihood of more randomized trials is slim, but argued that they were necessary to reduce biases in data.

"The bottom line is that there is no evidence there are better outcomes, but there is less blood loss and faster time to playing golf," Chodak said.

Instead of randomized trials, most research has been done through the less effective cohort studies, studies that follow people who chose their own treatment. Because the studies aren't randomized, it might, for example, turn out that the type of people who request da Vinci surgery are the people who do the most outside research into cancer treatments and are most likely to pursue other effective lifestyle changes. But even the cohort studies do not peg da Vinci as a universal panacea.

"It's a new technology and there's certainly surgeons and hospitals that are pushing the technology and describing it in a way to make it sound better. If that's what people are told, that's what people believe," Hodin said.

Robotic Surgery Is Not Cost Effective

Some robotic surgeries, such as the cystectomy (the removal of all or part of the bladder) did fare well in these studies. While the cost of a robot based procedure is always more expensive, that cost may be offset by the reduction in the hospital stay and fewer necessary corrective procedures.

A 2011 review study by researchers at the University of Bern in Switzerland and the University of Southern California noted that complications in cystectomies could add as much as $20,000 and that after one month complications were nearly 50 percent more likely in traditional, rather than robotic surgery. The Bern study speculated that cutting the costs of complications could compensate for the high price of the robotic procedure, though evidence of this is still pending.

But reduced complications do not result from all robotic procedures. A 2011 cohort study by the University of Modena and Reggio Emilia in Italy found that average length of hospital stays and number of surgical complications were almost identical in patients receiving traditional and robotic splenectomies (when all or part of the spleen is removed). The study of 90 patients found that the total cost of robotic spleen surgeries was nearly three times as much as conventional surgeries.

Still, it's difficult to argue with testimonials from people like Wright, who chose to go through with the surgery and was pleased with the results. "There's no question in my mind that if you're a surgical candidate, it's a good alternative if you have a well-trained physician doing it."

He said to choose the technician—not the technique, which may ultimately be the main thing fans and detractors of robotic surgery can agree on.

> *"New consumer tools have made self-tracking both simpler and more rigorous, generating reams of data that can be scrutinized for patterns and clues."*

Self-Tracking Technology Can Help People Live Healthier Lives

Emily Singer

In the following viewpoint, a medical journalist describes the advancements in direct-to-consumer medical technology that have made it possible for patients to better track their health information. For some, self-tracking is a lifestyle; for others, it is life saving, according to the author. Being able to aggregate self-tracked data, she maintains, has helped some groups test emerging treatments. The biggest challenge to self-tracking, she claims, is garnering widespread usage, a problem companies are trying to mitigate by incorporating self-tracking into social media. Emily Singer is the senior biomedicine editor for the Massachusetts Institute of Technology's Technology Review.

As you read, consider the following questions:

1. According to Singer, what affordable device is being used by self-trackers to track their sleep cycles?
2. How does the new generation of self-tracking tools operate to keep costs low, as described by Singer?
3. According to Singer, how have companies combined self-tracking and social networking to appeal to users?

On a quiet Wednesday night in April, an unusual group has assembled in a garage turned hacker studio nestled in a student-dominated neighborhood outside Boston. Those gathered here—mostly in their 20s or 30s and mostly male—are united by a deep interest in themselves. They have come to share the results or their latest self-experiments: monthlong tests of the Zeo, a consumer device designed to analyze sleep.

The group is part of a rapidly growing movement of fitness buffs, techno-geeks, and patients with chronic conditions who obsessively monitor various personal metrics. At the center of the movement is a loosely organized group known as the Quantified Self, whose members are driven by the idea that collecting detailed data can help them make better choices about their health and behavior. In meetings held all over the world, self-trackers discuss how they use a combination of traditional spreadsheets, an expanding selection of smart-phone apps, and various consumer and custom-built devices to monitor patterns of food intake, sleep, fatigue, mood, and heart rate.

Self-Tracking Is Supported by Consumer Technology

Of course, self-tracking is not new. Many athletes have been meticulously monitoring personal metrics for decades. And some people with chronic conditions such as migraines, diabetes, and allergies have done the same in an effort to shed light on how daily habits may influence their symptoms. But new consumer tools have made self-tracking both simpler and more rigorous, generating reams of data that can be scrutinized for patterns and clues. The new devices, along with the increasing ease of sharing data with other users through social-networking sites, mean that more and more people are finding it useful to quantify their lives. The Zeo, a $199 device based on technology that until recently required the services of a trained technician, makes it easy for users to track their sleep cycles. The device consists of a soft headband with a fabric sensor that wirelessly transmits EEG [electroencephalogram] data to a bedside monitor. A programmable alarm clock wakes the wearer at the optimal phase of sleep. And each night's data can be uploaded to a computer, where users can study how their sleep is affected by environmental factors such as weather, light, and more.

Self-Tracking Sleep Patterns

Sanjiv Shah, a longtime insomniac who participates in the Boston group, believes that wearing orange-tinted glasses for several hours before bed makes it easier for him to fall asleep. (The theory is that the orange tint blocks blue light, which has been shown in both human and animal studies to influence circadian rhythms.) To quantify the effects, he used not only the Zeo but also a thumb-size device called the Fitbit, which incorporates an accelerometer that measures movement, and a camera trained on his bed to record his sleep for a month. His results: without the glasses, he took an average of 28 minutes to fall asleep, but with them he took only four.

The experiment has an obvious flaw: Shah knows when he is wearing the glasses, and he believes they work, so the placebo effect could be responsible for their success. Matt Bianchi, a neurologist at Massachusetts General Hospital who spoke at the get-together, says no large-scale studies have shown that orange glasses improve sleep. (By the end of the evening, plans for a group experiment to test the technique were underway.) But self-trackers say the idea of reproducing the results in scientific tests misses the point. The glasses clearly work for Shah. And an $8 pair of plastic glasses is certainly preferable to sleep drugs as a way to gain that benefit.

As Gary Wolf, a journalist and cofounder of the Quantified Self, puts it, "It's a trial that begins with one very important person: yourself."

Self-Trackers Come Together

Over Memorial Day weekend, approximately 400 hackers, programmers, designers, engineers, and health-care professionals gathered at the Computer History Museum, in the tech mecca of Mountain View, California, for the first annual Quantified Self conference. Attendees showed off fitness monitors, apps to gather and display data, and even a set of sticker sensors with embedded accelerometers to detect movement, which are designed to be stuck on toothbrushes, water bottles, or a dog's leash.

Standing out in the crowd was Alex Gilman, a researcher at Fujitsu Laboratories of America, who ambled down the main hall with a bag slung over his shoulder. A tangle of wires sprouting from it led to monitors on different parts of his body: a white plastic ear clip, which measured his blood oxygen levels; a blood pressure cuff around his arm; and a combination heart rate monitor, EKG, temperature gauge, and accelerometer strapped to his chest. The bag itself held a prototype device designed to gather and synchronize the data from all those sensors and analyze it with the help of new algorithms.

The devices are a taste of the not-so-distant future, when the monitoring tools now typical of a hospital's intensive-care unit will be transformed into wearable gadgets that are unobtrusive and effortless to use. Gilman's chest strap is from a company called Zephyr, which has traditionally made equipment to track the physiology of military personnel and emergency workers during stressful situations. Zephyr is developing simplified consumer versions of its products; the latest one tracks motion, heart rate, and respiration and includes software to assess the user's fitness level. The blood pressure cuff and the clip to measure blood oxygen, which come from different manufacturers, are still too bulky to incorporate into consumer devices. The data, however, can be integrated into a single online dashboard with the help of Zephyr software.

Improving Quality of Life Through Self-Tracking

The new generation of devices relies on inexpensive, low-power wireless transceivers that can automatically send data to the wearer's cell phone or computer. Compared with the limited snapshot of health that is captured during an annual visit to the doctor's office, these tools and techniques could reveal the measures of someone's health "in context, and with a much richer resolution," says Paul Tarini, a senior program officer at the Robert Wood Johnson Foundation, which donated $64,000 to help the Quantified Self group create a guide to self-tracking tools.

Wearable sensors that measure vital signs such as blood pressure and heart rhythm around the clock could lead to applications we haven't thought of yet, says cardiologist Eric Topol, director of the Scripps Institute for Translational Medicine. Perhaps they could help people get a handle on health concerns such as headaches or fatigue, which don't qualify as diseases but can have a huge effect on quality of life. "People often get lightheaded in daily activities," Topol says. "Is that symptom linked to an abnormal heart rhythm? Are headaches linked to abnormally high blood pressure?"

Closing the Gap Between Collecting and Analyzing Data

At the Quantified Self conference, the museum's walls were lined with posters describing personalized dashboards and other apps for collecting and aggregating data. But tools for analyzing the data are much harder to come by. That's why Gilman and collaborators at Fujitsu built the device in his shoulder bag. One application they've developed is a way to use time-stamped raw data from wearable blood pressure monitors to make sure readings aren't taken when the user is active, which can yield misleading results. The new software tells the device to calculate blood pressure only when another monitor reveals that the wearer has been sitting still, as indicated by a steady heart rate.

The Fujitsu researchers are especially excited about using information collected instantaneously from the EKG to calculate heart rate variability, a well-validated indicator of stress. Taking a reading with previous instruments requires the subject to stand or sit still for several minutes, says Dave Marvit, vice president of the Connected Information Innovation Center at Fujitsu Laboratories of America. That makes it difficult to monitor stress as people go about their daily lives. Recently, Marvit tested the algorithm while moving naturally during an online game of speed chess. A graph charting his stress level in real time showed a spike as he contemplated a move to throw off his opponent's strategy, and a drop as he relaxed with the satisfaction of winning the game. "Seeing the physiological consequences of the mental state makes it much more real," he says. "It's much more interesting to measure stress while you're living your life than when you're standing still."

Self-Tracking Data Contributes to Research

Perhaps the most interesting consequences of the self-tracking movement will come when its adherents merge their findings into databases. The Zeo, for example, gives its users the option of making anonymized data available for research; the result is a database orders of magnitude larger than any other repository of information on sleep stages. Given that the vast majority of our knowledge about sleep—including the idea that eight hours is optimal—comes from highly controlled studies, this type of database could help to redefine healthy sleep behavior. Sleep patterns may be much more variable than is currently thought. Zeo

The Benefits of Self-Tracking

Taking advantage of new wearable wireless devices that can measure things like sleep patterns, walking speeds, heart rates, and even calories consumed and expended, more and more people are signing up to download and analyze their personal data. Nearly 10 million such devices will be sold in North America in 2011, according to the market forecasting company ABI Research.

Most self-trackers are extreme fitness buffs or—like [Google software engineer Bob] Evans—technology pioneers inherently interested in novel software applications. But Evans believes that personal data collecting could have stunning payoffs that go beyond just taking a better measure of everyday behavior. Already, some proponents claim personal benefits from logging their habits—eliminating foods that trigger migraines or upset stomachs, for instance, or saving certain tasks for their most productive time of day. Applied more broadly, data collected by self-trackers could help them find better treatments for diseases and even predict illness before symptoms become obvious.

Kate Greene, "Our Data, Ourselves,"
Discover, *December 8, 2011.*
discovermagazine.com.

researchers have already found that women get less REM sleep than men and are now analyzing whether the effect of aging on sleep differs by sex. The database is obviously biased, given that it is limited to people who bought the Zeo; those people are mostly men, with ample income and presumably some sleep-related concerns. But the sample is still probably at least as diverse as the population of the typical sleep study. Bianchi, who studies a number of sleep disorders and is developing his own home sleep-tracking tool, says an individualized approach to the study of sleep may help shed light on its complexities. "I have become skeptical of sleep science and clinical trials, so I am very interested in what individuals have to say," he says.

Patient Groups Share Data and Improve Treatments

There are plenty of reasons to believe that people sharing data about themselves can produce powerful medical insights. Patient groups formed around specific diseases have been among the first to recognize the benefits to be derived from aggregating such information and sharing it.

In 2004, Alexandra Carmichael, a longtime migraine sufferer, identified dairy and gluten as the triggers for her headaches after extensively tracking her pain and correlating it with diet and other factors. Hoping to help others find relief from chronic pain, she founded CureTogether, a social-networking site where patients can list their symptoms, the treatments they have tried, and the results they've observed. Aggregating and analyzing the information has begun to reveal broader trends. For example, Carmichael and other members of CureTogether found evidence that people who experience vertigo with their migraines are four times more likely to see their pain increase than decrease if they take Imitrex, a migraine medication that constricts blood vessels. In the near term, new members to the site can use this information to help decide which treatments to try first. In the longer term, scientists studying migraines could explore this link more formally.

Such studies obviously lack the rigor of clinical trials, but they have their own advantages. Clinical trials usually impose stringent criteria, excluding people who have conditions or take medications other than the one being studied. But self-tracking studies often include such people so their pool of participants may better reflect the actual patient population.

The Use of Self-Tracking in Clinical Trials

PatientsLikeMe, a social-networking site that provides users with tools to track their health status and communicate with other patients, has gathered a wealth of data on its 105,000 members. (The site makes money by anonymizing the data and selling it to pharmaceutical companies and other customers.) In 2008, after a small Italian study published in the *Proceedings of the National Academy of Sciences* suggested that lithium could delay the progression of ALS, or Lou Gehrig's disease, a small group of the ALS patients on PatientsLikeMe began taking the drug, and the company rolled out a number of tools to help them track their symptoms, their respiratory capacity, their dosage and blood levels of lithium, and any side effects they observed. Because the patients had collected so much data on themselves before starting the drug, researchers could analyze how their symptoms changed in the 12 months before they began taking it as well [as] studying any changes that came after—something that's not possible in the typical clinical trial. The company published a study based on its data in April. The drug, unfortunately, was found to have no effect.

Self-Tracking Could Result in Personalized Medicine

The growing availability of new monitoring devices and the increasing sophistication of social networks promise to make self-tracking much more powerful than it was when patients who wanted to monitor their own conditions were limited to standard spreadsheets and daily logs. "We see the potential to change the power dynamics in health care," says the Robert Wood Johnson Foundation's Tarini. People could take far more responsibility for monitoring their own health. The concept of personalized medicine could change as well; rather than relying on pharmaceutical companies that have little incentive to individualize treatments, patients could simply try different interventions and record how their physiological signs and symptoms change in response.

Of course, it remains to be seen whether a movement rooted in individual experimentation can scale up in ways that will affect public health. Even if it has the potential to do so, incorporating findings of this type into the health-care system is likely to be an enormous challenge. When you start with information from a study of one person, says Tarini, "the system doesn't have a way of determining what should be explored further." And because many of the new tools for tracking are aimed at consumers rather than the medical market, they have not undergone the rigorous testing required of medical devices. Still, Tarini is optimistic. "We have the opportunity to explore a whole new set of information," he says. "That has the potential to teach us a lot about health care."

The Big Payoff of Self-Tracking

The early adopters of self-tracking are often odd. In one breakout session at the May conference, a group earnestly discussed the results of their experiments. Standing on one leg for eight minutes a day helped one person sleep. Eating butter helped another think better. One had logged every line of computer code he'd written for a decade. But there is a far more pragmatic side to the movement, too. Across the building from the butter eater, another group, made up mostly of entrepreneurs, discussed business models for selling self-tracking apps and devices.

The favored strategy of the moment is to weave together self-tracking tools with social networks and gaming, using the lessons of behavioral economics to keep users motivated enough to meet any health goals they've set for themselves. "We want to create an engaging device that makes people want to make better health choices," says Julie Wilner, product director at Basis, a startup developing a new watch laden with sensors. "We do that by tracking data and showing it on the Web and on mobile devices, and by sharing it with friends."

The Ultimate Goal of Self-Tracking

Withings, a French company that makes wireless scales and blood pressure monitors, gives users the option of tweeting their weight, with the goal of adding social pressure to make people stick to a diet (Only a small percentage of users employ that feature, and the vast majority of them are men. The company is also experimenting with delaying readings from the scale. That way, the user may be less likely to get discouraged on a bad day and stop weighing herself.) And Green Goose, the startup developing the sensor-equipped stickers for household objects, plans to create a game based on personal health goals, awarding points whenever the user walks the dog or takes vitamins.

Yet even as startups plot how to profit from the trend, the people behind the self-tracking movement have a very different mind-set—and very different goals. "I find that the most interesting tools are those that give us the chance to reflect on who we are," says Wolf, the Quantified Self founder. The problems self-tracking tries to solve, he says, are important to everyone's life: "How to eat, how to sleep, how to learn, how to work, how to be happy."

> "Google Health failed largely because consumers did not see the value of a PHR [personal health record] and because it was time-consuming to input data."

People Do Not Use Self-Tracking Technology Enough to Realize Health Benefits

Kent Bottles

In the following viewpoint, a physician argues that projects like Google Health—implemented to help people self-track their health data—failed because Google misunderstood consumer interest and gave up too soon. He contends that before the ubiquity of smartphones, smaller sensors, social media, and cloud technology, self-tracking was too time-consuming. However, he maintains that advances in social media have made self-tracking the new frontier of establishing healthy habits. Kent Bottles is a blogger and a healthcare leadership consultant.

As you read, consider the following questions:

1. What is the World Health Organization's definition of health, according to Bottles, and how does it differ from what is generally taught in medical school?

2. According to the author, what surprising activity did Dr. Joseph Kvedar discover burned more calories than bicycling?

3. According to Bottles, what theory of disease emerged from studying social networks?

*T*o *measure is to know.*
   —Lord Kelvin

If you can not measure it, you can not improve it.
   —Lord Kelvin

Versus:

Asking science to explain life and vital matters is equivalent to asking a grammarian to explain poetry.
   —Nassim Nicholas Taleb

Technology is at its best when it is invisible.
   —Nassim Nicholas Taleb

How can technology help us live healthier lives? Why did Google Health fail? Why are Klout and Twitter Grader publicly issuing a number to me by name about how influential I am? What do Lord Kelvin and Nassim Nicholas Taleb have to teach us?

The Varying Definitions of Health

I was taught in medical school and pathology residency that health was defined as absence of disease; this definition pleased me because not much important could happen to the patient until I peered into my microscope and rendered a diagnosis. I looked up to Virchow and Rokitansky who were the most important and influential physicians in the most advanced medical centers in the 19th century.

In the mid-20th century the World Health Organization (WHO) famously stated: "Health is a state of complete physical, mental, and social well-being, and not merely the absence of disease or injury."

"The dialogue between Asclepios, the god of medicine, and Hygieia, the goddess of health—the external intervention and the well-lived life—goes back to the beginning. Only in the twentieth century did the triumph of 'scientific' modes of inquiry in medicine (as in most walks of life) result in the eclipse of Hygieia. Knowledge has increasingly become defined in terms of that (and only that) which emerges from the application of reductionist methods of investigation."

The WHO rejection of the "absence of disease" definition of health has been warmly embraced by some and largely ignored by many more. After all if the WHO definition means that our wellness is affected by all human activities, what should the Department of Health and Human Services focus on and budget for? The WHO definition of health has "been honoured in repetition, but rarely in application."

Why Google Health Failed

At one time I thought Google Health would become the Personal Health Record (PHR) that would allow individual patients to keep track of their medical and daily activity data and apply the WHO definition of health to their own life; I blogged about PHRs because I hoped they would solve the enormous problem of hospital based IT systems not communicating with each other.

I still remember the excitement when Google CEO Eric Schmidt described Google Health for the first time at HIMSS 2008, and I played around with it. I found it easy to use and understand, but I never really used it for my own health and wellness purposes. The *Wall Street Journal* had a similar experience: "We signed up for Google Health . . . and a bunch of other personal health records for a story, but never quite felt compelled to actually use them."

Google Health failed because:

- Patients are not that interested in entering their data into a PHR
- Google underestimated the complexity of health care
- Most consumer health data is not in a structured, machine computable format
- As an untethered PHR, professionals distrusted the accuracy of the data
- Google did not work with or engage physicians in the effort
- It did not coordinate with technology developers

Self-Tracking Is Hard to Follow

Because I am no longer protecting the narrow interests of pathology, the WHO definition of health continues to ring true. Since all human activity affects health and wellness and since we have such poor memories, how does one better understand one's own body and mood? The personal informatics and quantified self movements are true descendants of Lord Kelvin; they believe that scientific, objective, quantified measurements can lead to behavior change that can promote wellness and health.

Dr. Joseph Kvedar changed his attitude about yard work when the data from his Bodymedia armband convinced him that he burned more calories doing gardening than bicycling. Shaun Ranee used the anonymous website drinkingdiary.com to reduce his drinking after his father received a diagnosis of end-stage liver disease. Jon Cousins built Moodscope, a self-tracking system to manage his bipolar affective disorder; he even shares his personal mood data with a few friends. His self-tracking metrics are supplemented by human sympathy made possible by his online connections and community.

While much that is written about self-tracking celebrates the potential of measurement to help the individual with sleep, exercise, sex, food, weight loss, mood, alertness, productivity, and spiritual well being, there is a dark side to the movement. Alexandra

Carmichael, one of the founders of CureTogether where patients conduct research on diseases, wrote about why she stopped monitoring 40 measurements about herself: "Each day my self-worth was tied to the data. One pound heavier this morning? You're fat. Skipped a day of running? You're lazy. It felt [like] being back in school. Less than 100 percent on an exam? You're dumb."

Google Health failed largely because consumers did not see the value of a PHR and because it was time-consuming to input data. Gary Wolf thinks four things have changed that make self-tracking easier and more acceptable:

- Electronic sensors got smaller and better
- People carry smartphones that are powerful computers
- Social media made it normal to share everything
- The development of the cloud

How Social Networking Affects Health

Other researchers believe that technology may support health and wellness not having individuals self-track, but by monitoring our social networks. This approach has been called the social contagion theory of disease, and much can be learned without the individual doing anything except carrying around his smartphone.

By analyzing the famous Framingham Heart Study, Nicholas A. Christakis and James H. Fowler were able to map 5,124 subjects for a connection web of 53,228 ties between families, friends, and co-workers. Obesity appears to spread among friends like a virus. "When a Framingham resident became obese, his or her friends were 57% more likely to become obese too." "A Framingham resident was roughly 20% more likely to become obese if the friend of a friend became obese." "You may not know him personally, but your friend's husband's co-worker can make you fat. And your sister's boyfriend can make you thin."

This social contagion process seems to also work for drinking, smoking, loneliness, and happiness. Christakis and Fowler believe that "these behaviors spread partly through the subconscious signals that we pick up from those around us, which serve as cues to what is considered normal behavior."

Alex Pentland, director of MIT's Human Dynamics Laboratory, uses cell phone data to identify the influences in any social network that are most likely to change other people's behaviors. Dr. Pentland says, "Just by watching where you spend time, I can say a lot about the music you like, the car you drive, your financial risk, your risk for diabetes. . . . We are trying to understand the molecules of behavior in this really complete way."

The Role of Social Media "Klout"

Although I have never been studied by MIT, I have been assigned a number that supposedly indicates how influential I am. According to Twitter Grader I am ranked 88,837th out of 9,826,593 with a grade of 100 out of 100. Klout states that I am a "pundit" with a score of 69 out of 100. PeerIndex gives me a score of 18. What do these numbers really mean? I have no idea.

"Now you are being assigned a number in a very public way, whether you want it or not," said Mark W. Schaefer of Rutgers University. More than 2,500 companies are now using Klout data, and special offers are just starting to come into my email box. The CEO of Klout of course thinks this is a great idea: "For the first time, we're all on an even playing field. For the first time, it's not just how much money you have or what you look like. It's what you say and how you say it." Others are not so sure and worry about creating social media caste systems and that such rating systems lack sentiment analysis (negative comments can be as effective as positive comments in raising one's score).

Seeking the Next Personal Health Record

So what can we conclude from this dizzying tour of health, wellness, measurement, technology, and life? I think we need both

Lord Kelvin and Nassim Nicholas Taleb to guide us. I think it is a mistake to choose the WHO definition over the absence of disease definition of health, as though they are polar opposites. There is a continuum of meanings for the word health. "At one end of that continuum is well-being in the broadest sense, the all-encompassing definition of the WHO, almost a Platonic ideal of the Good. At the other end is the simple absence of negative biological circumstances—disease, pain, disability, or death."

I think Google will in the future realize they shut down Google Health too soon. As smartphones and sensors make it easier and easier to automatically input data, people will want a place to store all of their observations of daily living and medical data.

Gaming for Health

Taleb is right; technology is at its best when it is invisible. However, some of the most important things in life are not reducible to a number or a PowerPoint slide with bullet points. Twitter Grader says I am 100 out of 100; Klout 69 out of 100; and PeerIndex 18 out of 100. Not all of these rankings can be accurately measuring my influence to my Twitter community and readers of my blog. And let's not forget what we are learning from social contagion theory; it is not just about the individual. I also think that there may be something to the [health start-up] Keas approach which, as I understand it tries to use game theory to make it more fun to use technology to help us change unhealthy behaviors. Tom Chatfield's *Fun Inc: Why Gaming Will Dominate the Twenty-First Century* and Jane McGonigal's *Reality Is Broken: Why Games Make Us Better and How They Can Change the World* certainly gave me many ideas about how to create flow for human beings in the service of individual and population health.

> *"Most of the data on ionizing radiation comes from victims of the atomic bomb attacks on Hiroshima and Nagasaki, and . . . they do not apply to diagnostic radiation."*

Medical Physicists Say Fear of Diagnostic Radiation Is Overblown

Joel N. Shurkin

In the following viewpoint, a journalist examines the controversy surrounding a statement supporting diagnostic technology—including radiation imagery—by the American Association of Physicists in Medicine. The author outlines the relative safety of diagnostic radiation and claims the health benefits of diagnostic imaging far outweigh the relatively low doses of radiation. Joel N. Shurkin is a Baltimore-based freelance writer. He was part of a team of writers who won the Pulitzer Prize for their coverage of the Three Mile Island nuclear reactor disaster.

As you read, consider the following questions:

1. According to Shurkin, what dosage of radiation is deemed too low to be detectable by the American Association of Physicists in Medicine?

Joel N. Shurkin, "Medical Physicists Say Fear of Diagnostic Radiation Is Overblown," *Inside Science News Service*, January 11, 2012. www.insidescience.org. Reprinted with permission from Inside Science News Service. Copyright © 2012, American Institute of Physics.

2. How many people, according to Shurkin, undergo computed tomography (CT) scans each year?

3. How many millisieverts of radiation does a person receive from a full-body CT scan, as described in the viewpoint?

An association of physicists in the medical field has warned patients not to decline diagnostic radiation procedures because of perceptions that the tests may be harmful.

The American Association of Physicists in Medicine said the benefits of diagnostic—mostly imaging—technology far outweighed the risks. Machines that deliver much higher levels of radiation for treating cancer have been the subject of media stories uncovering improper use and accidents, and journal articles have cautioned physicians to minimize diagnostic CT scans in children, especially repeated ones. They have raised unfounded fears about radiation procedures in general, the association said.

The statement touched on a long-debated topic: whether all radiation is bad or if some of it can be tolerated without danger.

"Discussion of risks related to radiation dose from medical imaging procedures should be accompanied by acknowledgment of the benefits of the procedures. Risks of medical imaging at effective doses below 50 mSv (millisieverts) for single procedures or 100 mSv for multiple procedures over short time periods are too low to be detectable and may be nonexistent," said the statement released by the AAPM. "Predictions of hypothetical cancer incidence and deaths in patient populations exposed to such low doses are highly speculative and should be discouraged."

The statement was issued because of concern that papers in scientific journals, warning against dangers from CT scans, were finding their way into the popular media, and "people became fearful and said they were not going to have the exams," said William Hendee of the Medical College of Wisconsin, lead author of the AAPM statement. That was particularly true of parents of children slated for exams.

Hendee said that most of the data on ionizing radiation comes from victims of the atomic bomb attacks on Hiroshima and Nagasaki, and that they do not apply to diagnostic radiation.

The statement was immediately criticized by scientists who think almost any radiation can produce harmful effects, particularly cancer.

"It's a very blasé, a surprising statement from people whose job it is to ensure the safety of what we do," said Rebecca Smith-Bindman, a professor of radiology and several other medical departments at the University of California at San Francisco. "Ionizing radiation is the most studied carcinogen in the world."

Smith-Bindman added that the literature shows a risk for solid tumors and leukemia—even at low exposure—although the lower the exposure, the less certain the risk, and that the fear that patients would decline needed CT scans was "unjustified."

"Seventy-five million people—one in four—have CT scans every year," Smith-Bindman said. "Few refused necessary exams."

The debate over radiation safety goes back to the discovery of radiation in 1895, and is one of the frustrating instances in which medical experts do not agree.

Radiation is measured in sieverts, which is the amount of energy deposited in living tissue. A full-body CT scan results in 12 mSv; a mammogram 0.13 mSv—a hundred times less. The risks from these procedures, according to AAPM, are too low to have been determined reliably, and may be "nonexistent."

The risk factor is a matter of extrapolation.

According to a study quoted by the National Academy of Sciences, a 45-year-old adult undergoing 30 annual full-body CT scans would have one chance in 50 of dying of cancer because of the radiation. Almost no one would have that many procedures. The odds of a person born in 1999 dying from a car crash is one in 77.

"Thanks to your microwave leaking radiation . . . !" cartoon by Jack Crobett. www.Car toonStock.com. Copyright © Jack Crobett. Reproduction rights obtainable from www .CartoonStock.com.

The academy said that there would be one cancer caused by a single exposure per hundred people of 100 mSv, more than a single CT scan would put out. Of those 100 people, 42 would have solid tumors and leukemia from other causes in their lifetime.

The devices discussed are machines used for diagnosis of disease, not treatment, which uses much higher doses.

Scientists disagree as to whether there is a threshold below which there is no risk. Most experts, including the national academy, accept a "linear no-threshold model" which states that the less the radiation, the less the risk but there is no completely safe threshold.

The problem, said Daniel Low, science council chair of AAPM, is that extrapolation for very low dose assessments of cancers or death, is "inaccurate, unscientific and leads to concern by patients." Such predictions of cancer and deaths from low doses are "speculative," AAPM says in its statement.

People don't understand the uncertainties, Low said.

The situation is made worse by journalists who confuse relative risk with absolute risk in their stories. If the mortality of a disease increases from two persons per 100,000 to four per 100,000, it is true that the relative risk has doubled, but the absolute risk remains very low.

"I wish that all journalists, including science journalists, did a better job of reporting on risk, of making sure that our stories always were set within a realistic perspective," said Deborah Blum, a Pulitzer-Prize winning science writer who now teaches at the University of Wisconsin at Madison. "Far too often we end up scaring people unnecessarily or focusing attention on unlikely risk scenarios and distracting from the major ones. . . . Journalists as a pack tend to pick up the different, the dramatic, the one in a million chance of mortality."

Other organizations seem to agree with the AAPM statement.

"We believe that risk of radiation exposure from diagnostic imaging is much less than the risk of not having the examination if the examination is diagnostically warranted," said Penny Butler, senior director at the American College of Radiology.

Mary Mahoney, chair of public information at the Radiological Society of North America and a radiologist at the University of Cincinnati Medical Center, said her organization agrees completely with AAPM and is revising its position on its website to link to the AAPM.

"I don't want anyone not to get critically important information because of fear of the radiation," said Mahoney.

Smith-Bindman said part of the problem is that sometimes the devices are used when they are not necessary, a situation peculiar to the American medical system. In the United Kingdom and Europe the devices are not used unless the need is warranted by the patient's medical condition.

On that, everyone seems to agree.

"[AAPM] acknowledges that medical imaging procedures should be appropriate and conducted at the lowest radiation dose consistent with acquisition of the desired information," the organization said in a press release.

> *"All ionizing radiation passes unimpeded through cells of the body, mutating or destroying DNA along the way."*

Medical Imaging Exposes People to Too Much Radiation

Shannon Brownlee and Sam Wainwright

In the following viewpoint, two health researchers detail the rise in computed tomography (CT) scans. According to the authors, studies indicate that CT scans cause 29,000 cancers per year and 14,500 deaths. The reason for the increase in CT scans, they claim, is driven by money and demanding patients. Shannon Brownlee is the director of the New America Foundation Health Policy Program. Sam Wainwright is a research associate with the New America Foundation Health Policy Program and an editor for New Health Dialogue.

As you read, consider the following questions:

1. According to the authors, what is the annual limit of exposure for US radiation workers?
2. By what percent, write Brownlee and Wainwright, has the number of CT scans increased over the past fifteen years?

3. In 2006, how many people had a full-body CT scan to look for early signs of cancer, according to the viewpoint?

There's an eerie video up on YouTube, shot by a Japanese journalist who ventured into the evacuation zone surrounding the Fukushima nuclear power plant, armed with a camera and a radiation meter. The video looks like b-roll footage from a low-budget zombie movie, with roving bands of stray dogs and a soundtrack of the radiation meter's increasingly frantic beeping.

Shortly after the earthquake that damaged the plant, the Japanese government evacuated residents from a more than 1,000 square mile zone. Last week, [May 2011] they raised the severity level of the crisis at Fukushima to a 7 out of 7, making it the worst nuclear disaster since the complete meltdown of the reactor at Chernobyl, in 1986. In its wake, worldwide fear of nuclear power spiked. The German government shut down seven of its 17 nuclear reactors, and plans to eliminate nuclear power by 2020. In the U.S., a Fox News Poll conducted in early April found that 83 percent of respondents thought a similar disaster could happen to an American nuclear plant.

What Radiation Does to the Body

People fear radiation for good reason. All ionizing radiation passes unimpeded through cells of the body, mutating or destroying DNA along the way. The danger level depends on the dose and the length of exposure. We're exposed to small amounts of radiation all the time—from cosmic rays to the normal radioactive decay of soil, rocks and building materials. Even the granite in the U.S. Capitol Building emits low levels of radiation. These levels are harmless, but a high dose can kill, and prolonged or repeated moderate exposure can lead to cancer.

Patients Are Willing to Be Exposed

So why are we afraid of nuclear power, but not worried about the radiation in medical imaging tests, such as a CT [computed tomography] scan? Here are a couple of scenarios to contemplate. Imagine waking up in the middle of the night, drenched in sweat, with an unfamiliar tightness in your chest. It could be a panic attack—you're certainly feeling panicky in the moment—but maybe it's a heart attack, so you take yourself to the emergency room. Your tests look fine, but you're middle-aged with a gut and a smoking habit, so your doctor recommends you undergo a CT scan, just to be sure you don't have any dangerous plaque building up in your coronary arteries.

Now let's imagine a different situation. This time when you wake up in the middle of the night, it's an earthquake that jolts you out of bed, and you're a worker at the local nuclear power plant. You get a call from your supervisor, ordering you to suit up and get yourself down to the plant, which has been damaged by the quake and may be leaking radiation.

One choice seem like a no-brainer—getting that CT scan—while the other seems like a walk into the jaws of death, yet in both cases you would be exposed to similar amounts of radiation, about 15 millisieverts. (A millisievert is one of several ways to measure the dose of radiation.)

The Dangers of Diagnostic Imaging

Other imaging tests deliver an even bigger blast. Inserting a stent, a little metal tube used to prop open a coronary artery, involves CT angiography, a kind of x-ray movie, and it can deliver up to 57 millisieverts during the course of one imaging test. That's the equivalent of standing at the power plant's gates for almost 5 hours during the peak of the crisis. 50 millisieverts is the annual limit for U.S. radiation workers. A cumulative dose of 100 millisieverts is known to increase the risk of cancer.

Radiation's harmful effects on the body are the same no matter the source, yet we see some kinds of radiation as bad and others as good. We request CT scans from doctors, but we'd have to be dragged kicking and screaming into the Fukushima evacuation zone.

Part of the reason for this is that the medical benefits of radiation can outweigh the harms. Before CT was used in medicine, beginning in the 1970s, a patient who suffered a blow to the head could be bleeding inside his brain, and there was no way to tell for sure without opening the skull, a surgery nobody wanted to do unless it was absolutely necessary. CT allowed doctors to peer through skin and bone and "see" soft tissue. Today, CT imaging is used to diagnose conditions ranging from brain bleeds to appendicitis to coronary artery disease.

Diagnostic Imaging May Be Causing Cancer

Yet, for all the benefits CT imaging offers, it's still radiation, some in the American medical community worry radiological imaging is causing cancer. The number of CT scans performed has risen about 10 percent annually over the last 15 years, while the U.S. population has increased by only about 1 percent a year. Doctors performed over 70 million CT scans last year, or one scan for every fifth person, increasing our annual per-capita radiation dose by 600 percent since 1980. Obviously some people are not getting any scans, which means others are getting a much bigger dose of radiation. Radiation exposure falls heavily on particular patient sets—those with heart problems, and those with breasts.

This rapid expansion of CT is undoubtedly causing cancers. Recent studies suggest CT causes 29,000 cases of cancer a year, leading to 14,500 deaths. To put that in perspective, an equal number of people die from ovarian cancer each year. CT scanning is a real and significant cause of death.

Incidents of Radiation Overexposure

In addition to the slowly accumulating danger of repeated radiation exposure, cases continue to come to light detailing overdoses from medical imaging errors. In 2009, more than 200 stroke patients at Cedars-Sinai Medical Center, in Los Angeles, began suffering from hair loss and skin redness after diagnostic head

CT Scans Are Linked to Cancer

The measure of an absorbed dose that can be dangerous from any source is about 50 mSv. [Stephen Amis Jr., chair of radiology at Albert Einstein College of Medicine and Montefiore Medical Center in the Bronx, New York] says, "The definitive study on this issue was in an article by Brenner and Hall published in the *New England Journal of Medicine* in 2007. They estimated that 1.5% to 2% of all cancers are due to CT scans alone, which came to 28,000 new cases of cancer every year.

"I really strongly believe in the risks of excessive radiation," Amis adds. "At our institution, we cut the number of CT exams by 5% last year."

*Thomas G. Dolan, "CT in the ER—
Radiologists and Emergency Physicians
Often See Radiation Risks and Benefits
Differently,"* Radiology Today, *vol. 12, no. 7,
July 2011, p. 16.*

CT scans, possible signs of acute radiation sickness. An FDA investigation found that technicians had blasted the patients with eight times the appropriate dose of radiation. The estimated exposure was approximately 3,000 to 4,000 millisieverts, the equivalent of 50,000 X-rays. According to the U.S. Nuclear Regulatory Commission, a dose of 3,500 millisieverts to the entire body is enough to kill a person.

The *New York Times* recently uncovered the case of Jacoby Roth, a 2½ year old boy who was brought to the emergency room in 2008 after falling out of bed. Over the next hour, the child was run through a CT scanner 151 times by a "rogue" radiology technician and suffered a massive radiation overdose of as much as 5,300 millisieverts to his brain.

While the academic community still debates the health effects of low radiation levels, there is growing evidence that children are at higher risk. Their smaller bodies are more sensitive to radiation than those of adults, and they have longer to live, which means more time to develop cancer. Kids are routinely exposed to adult doses of radiation, which can be twice as harmful to a young body. A head CT can deliver almost 100 millisieverts to the infant skull and operators consistently fail to adjust scanners to lower pediatric settings.

Putting Pressure on Physicians

Doctors are slowly waking up to the potential dangers posed by CT, but the number of scans continues to rise. Money is one reason. For every patient who passes through a scanner, the hospital makes money, helping them pay for their multi-million dollar machines. Some emergency physicians report being pressured by their hospitals to order CT scans. Doctors who own imaging centers are more likely to recommend scans than doctors who do not have a financial interest. In 2006, the latest year for which figures are available, 200,000 people submitted to a whole-body CT scan to look for early signs of several cancers. A whole-body CT delivers a whopping 25 millisieverts, and every credible medical group has condemned the practice.

Defensive medicine and demanding patients are two more compelling forces. Even when physicians know that a patient is better off without a scan, they worry about getting sued if the patient goes on to develop a condition that might have been spotted earlier. The cancer the patient may get down the road seems like a distant risk for the doctor. Patients also tend to focus on near-term dangers. Even if there's virtually no chance that your kid has suffered any harm after falling off the couch, a CT scan seems like the prudent decision, just to be sure he doesn't have a brain bleed. Our general obliviousness to the long-term risks of radiation makes it very difficult for physicians to convince us otherwise.

The Medical Device "Arms Race"

The medical device arms race has played a part. Hospitals regularly compete to have the most high-tech equipment, driven on by the importance placed on technology by the *U.S. [News] & World Report*'s hospital rankings. They advertise their newest gizmo to draw in patients, enthralled by the promise of safer, faster, (and the omnipotent and ambiguous) better. The assumption is made that the newest GE or Siemens' scanner provides an improvement in patient care. In the case of radiological imaging, as in an alarming amount of medicine more broadly, there are surprisingly few studies comparing patient outcomes between older, less dangerous techniques and the shiny new toy. It's not clear, for example, that the widespread use of abdominal CT scans has improved the diagnosis of appendicitis. Doctors don't know if the scans are helping to make patients any healthier, but continue to use them even though we know the increased levels of radiation they expose patients to can hurt and even kill them.

It took two concurrent acts of god—an earthquake plus a tsunami—to cause the crisis in Japan and expose the countryside to radiation levels deemed too dangerous to live with. In the U.S., all it takes is a poorly trained radiology technician, a persistent patient, or a defensive doctor. Unlike the handful of Japanese nuclear workers who have been exposed to sickening levels of radiation willingly as part of the known risks of their profession, American patients are exposed to equal risks unaware that they're often doing it for no good reason. As the ongoing disaster at the Fukushima power plant focuses the world's attention on the insidious dangers of radiation, maybe it's time to think just as hard about a CT scan as heading into the fallout zone of a nuclear disaster.

Periodical and Internet Sources Bibliography

The following articles have been chosen to supplement the diverse views presented in this chapter.

Diagnostic and Interventional Cardiology	"New Technology Allows CT Scans with Fraction of Current Radiation Dose," March 16, 2012. www.dicardiology.com.
Dave Fornell	"How Much CT Dose Did I Receive . . . Anyone?," *ITN: Imaging Technology News*, March 16, 2012. www.itnonline.com.
G.F.	"Down, And Roll Me 20," *Economist*, April 22, 2012. www.economist.com/blogs/babbage.
Chris Gullo	"Half of Doctors to Use Medical Apps in 2012," *Mobi Health News*, November 16, 2011. mobihealthnews.com.
Marina Koren	"How Raven, the Open-Source Surgical Robot, Could Change Medicine," *Popular Mechanics*, February 28, 2012.
Denise Mann	"Many Medical Tests, Procedures Not Always Needed," *WebMD Health News*, April 5, 2012. www.webmd.com/news.
Mariann Martin	"Thousands of Medical Apps Help Patients and Doctors Monitor Illness, But Overall Usage Remains Low," *Chattanooga Times Free Press*, March 17, 2012. www.timesfreepress.com.
Elizabeth Armstrong Moore	"Tiny Monitor Tracks Vital Signs Sans Skin Contact," *CNet News*, February 2, 2012. news.cnet.com.
Karen Weintraub	"Showing the Power of Molecular Self-Tracking," *Technology Review*, March 16, 2012. www.technologyreview.com.

CHAPTER 2

How Does Medical Technology Affect Health-Care Costs?

Chapter Preface

Advances in medical technology—such as defibrillators and x-rays—have increased life expectancy. Some argue that it is foolish to attempt to control costs through reducing medical technology because it may cost lives. Others argue that the soaring cost of health care in the United States leaves the poor and elderly with limited options, potentially also costing lives as medical issues are not adequately treated.

In a 2009 article about the overuse of medical technology by Katherine Hobson in *U.S. News & World Report*, Paul Ginsburg, president of the Center for Studying Health System Change, states, "I don't think we have a lot of technologies that aren't useful. Our issue is that some of them are valuable but applied too broadly." Some of the technologies labeled as useful but overused by Hobson include computed tomography (CT) angiograms, implantable cardioverter-defibrillators, and proton-beam therapy—all expensive and on the rise in application.

"Technology creep" is a term used to describe how a new medical device, approved for a small selection of high-risk patients, gradually begins to be used in lower-risk treatments, off-label, or as a preventative measure. If the new technology is costly, then the economic impact shifts from the limited application to broader use without any cost-benefit to patients or doctors.

"Technology is only relevant to those who can afford it," writes Morgan Housel on the website of The Motley Fool, a financial services company. Housel suggests a number of strategies to lower the cost of health care that emphasize a more thoughtful, engaged approach on the part of patients and doctors, including higher deductibles to engage patients in decision making, mandatory insurance, and preventative measures over medical treatment for problems like obesity.

In a 2012 *Daily Finance* article, Alex Planes argues that what is needed to improve the economics of health care is *more* medical technology. He contends that improvements in medical technology, including automation and robotics, will "make health care more effective and more affordable." Detractors continue to fret that doctors, worried about litigation, are ordering more tests and treatments than are needed, and therefore driving up the cost of health care.

Many factors are at play when examining the question of how medical technology affects health-care costs, including Medicare/Medicaid, taxing medical devices, and the development of new technology. In the following chapter, authors offer varying viewpoints on how medical technology affects the economics of modern health care and the ability of patients to afford treatment.

VIEWPOINT 1

> "Researchers generally agree that
> advances in medical technology have
> contributed to rising overall U.S. health
> care spending."

New Technology Is Driving Up the Cost of Health Care

Henry J. Kaiser Family Foundation

In the following viewpoint, a research foundation examines how medical technology affects the cost of health care. Sometimes new technology saves money by replacing expensive machinery or procedures, the foundation explains, while other times technology increases health-care costs by expanding the number of patients who can be treated. The foundation claims that the development of new medical technology is driven by consumers, health-care professionals, and corporations. A cost-effective approach, the foundation suggests, could bring the rising cost of health care under control through financial incentives to patients and doctors. The Kaiser Family Foundation is a nonprofit that conducts research and publishes reports about health-care issues in the United States.

"How Changes in Medical Technology Affect Health Care Costs—Snapshot," The Henry J. Kaiser Family Foundation, March 2007; adapted by the author(s). This information was reprinted with permission from the Henry J. Kaiser Family Foundation. The Kaiser Family Foundation, a leader in health policy analysis, health journalism and communication, is dedicated to filling the need for trusted, independent information on the major health issues facing our nation and its people. The Foundation is a non-profit private operating foundation, based in Menlo Park, California.

As you read, consider the following questions:

1. According to the viewpoint, what was the amount of health-care spending per capita in 2005?
2. In 2005, what percentage of the US gross domestic product was health care, according to the foundation?
3. How much was spent on health research in the United States in 2005, according to the foundation?

Health expenditures continue to grow very rapidly in the U.S. Since 1970, health care spending has grown at an average annual rate of 9.8%, or about 2.5 percentage points faster than the economy as measured by the nominal gross domestic product (GDP). Annual spending on health care increased from $75 billion in 1970 to $2.0 trillion in 2005, and is estimated to reach $4 trillion in 2015. As a share of the economy, health care has more than doubled over the past 35 years, rising from 7.2% of GDP in 1970 to 16.0% of GDP in 2005, and is projected to be 20% of GDP in 2015. Health care spending per capita increased from $356 in 1970 to $6,697 in 2005, and is projected to rise to $12,320 in 2015.[1]

The particularly rapid increases in health insurance premiums over the last few years have focused the health policy community on the issues of cost containment and health insurance affordability. A key question from policymakers is why spending on health care consistently rises more rapidly than spending on other goods and services. Health care experts point to the development and diffusion of medical technology as primary factors in explaining the persistent difference between health spending and overall economic growth, with some arguing that new medical technology may account for about one-half or more of real long-term spending growth. This [viewpoint] briefly describes what health policy analysts mean by medical technology and the mechanisms by which it affects the growth in health care costs.

What Is Medical Technology?

Broadly speaking, the term "medical technology" can be used to refer to the procedures, equipment, and processes by which medical care is delivered. Examples of changes in technology would include new medical and surgical procedures (e.g., angioplasty, joint replacements), drugs (e.g., biologic agents), medical devices (e.g., CT scanners, implantable defibrillators), and new support systems (e.g., electronic medical records and transmission of information, telemedicine).[2] There is very little in the field of medicine that does not use some type of medical technology and that has not been affected by new technology.

The Effect of Medical Technology on Treatments

Heart disease and its consequence, heart attack, is the leading cause of death in the U.S. and a good example of how new technology has changed the treatment and prevention of a disease over time. In the 1970s, cardiac care units were introduced, lidocaine was used to manage irregular heartbeat, beta-blockers were used to lower blood pressure in the first 3 hours after a heart attack, "clot buster" drugs began to be widely used, and coronary artery bypass surgery became more prevalent. In the 1980s, blood-thinning agents were used after a heart attack to prevent reoccurrences, beta-blocker therapy evolved from short-term therapy immediately after a heart attack to maintenance therapy, and angioplasty (minimally invasive surgery) was used after heart attack patients were stable. In the 1990s, more effective drugs were introduced to inhibit clot formation, angioplasty was used for treatment and revascularization along with stents to keep blood vessels open, cardiac rehabilitation programs were implemented sooner, and implantable cardiac defibrillators were used in certain patients with irregular heartbeats. In the 2000s, better tests became available to diagnose heart attack, drug-eluting stents were used, and new drug strategies were developed (aspirin, ACE inhibitors, beta-blockers, statins) for long-term management of heart attack and potential heart attack patients. From 1980–2000, the overall mortality rate from heart attack fell by almost half, from 345.2 to 186.0 per 100,000 persons.[3]

Another example of how advances in technology have changed health outcomes over time is in the treatment of pre-term babies, for which very little could be done in 1950. But by 1990, changes in technology, including special ventilators, artificial pulmonary surfactant to help infant lungs develop, neonatal intensive care, and steroids for mother and/or baby, helped decrease mortality to one-third its 1950 level, with an overall increase in life expectancy of about 12 years per low-birthweight baby.[4]

How Does New Medical Technology Affect Health-Care Costs?

While a particular new technology may either increase or decrease health care spending, researchers generally agree that, taken together, advances in medical technology have contributed to rising overall U.S. health care spending. [Social scientist Richard A.] Rettig describes how new medical technology affects the costs of health care through the following "mechanisms of action":[5]

- Development of new treatments for previously untreatable terminal conditions, including long-term maintenance therapy for treatment of such diseases as diabetes, end-stage renal disease, and AIDS;
- Major advances in clinical ability to treat previously untreatable acute conditions, such as coronary artery bypass graft;
- Development of new procedures for discovering and treating secondary diseases within a disease, such as erythropoietin to treat anemia in dialysis patients;
- Expansion of the indications for a treatment over time, increasing the patient population to which the treatment is applied;

- On-going, incremental improvements in existing capabilities, which may improve quality;
- Clinical progress, through major advances or by the cumulative effect of incremental improvements, that extends the scope of medicine to conditions once regarded as beyond its boundaries, such as mental illness and substance abuse.

Whether a particular new technology will increase or reduce total health expenditures depends on several factors. One is its impact on the cost of treating an individual patient. Does the new technology supplement existing treatment, or is it a full or partial substitute for current approaches? Do these changes result in higher or lower health spending for each patient treated? In looking at the impact on cost per patient, consideration needs to be given to whether the direct costs of the new technology include any effect on the use or cost of other health care services such as hospital days or physician office visits.

Innovation Can Drive Up Health-Care Costs

A second factor is the level of use that a new technology achieves (i.e., how many times is the new technology used?). Does the new technology extend treatment to a broader population?— examples would be innovations that address previously untreatable illness, diagnose new populations for existing treatments, or extend existing treatments to new conditions. New technologies can also reduce utilization—for example, new screening or diagnosis capacity that allows more targeted treatment. There also are temporal aspects to evaluating the impact of new technologies on costs. Some innovations, such as a new vaccine, may cost more immediately but may lead to savings down the road if the vaccine results in fewer people seeking more expensive treatment. New technologies also can extend life expectancy, which affects both the type and amount of health care that people use in their lifetime.

Evaluating the impact of new innovation can be complicated. For example, a case study that focuses on a single technology or disease may show cost savings based on the costs and benefits of the new technology if it replaces a more expensive technology and provides health improvements, while an analysis of health care system-wide costs may show cost increases if the new technology results in greater utilization than the old. A specific example is anesthesia, where substantial innovations have occurred in recent years. Better anesthetic agents and practices have reduced the burden of surgery on patients, producing faster patient recoveries, shorter hospital stays, and fewer medical errors. These changes reduce the cost per patient compared to surgery in the absence of these changes. At the same time, these innovations also make it possible to perform surgeries on patients who previously would have been considered too frail to undergo the surgery; this adds to the amount of health care that is delivered system-wide, thus perhaps increasing total health care spending.

Health-Care Spending Is a Tangled Web

It is not possible to directly measure the impact of new medical technology on total health care spending; innovation in the health care sector occurs continuously, and the impacts of different changes interrelate. The size of the health sector (16% of gross domestic product in 2005) and its diversity (thousands of procedures, products, and interventions) also render direct measurement impractical. Economists have used indirect approaches to try to estimate the impact of new technology on the cost of health care.[6] In an often-cited article, [economist Joseph P.] Newhouse estimates the impact of medical technology on health care spending by first estimating the impact of factors that can reasonably be accounted for (e.g., spread of insurance, increasing per capita income, aging of the population, supplier-induced demand, low medical sector productivity gains). He concludes that the factors listed above account for well under half of the growth in real medical spending, and that the bulk of the unexplained

Cost-Savings of New Technology Is Not Passed on to the Patient

In most cases, as technology improves, prices go down. Prices of computers, flat screen televisions, and DVD players have fallen over time as their technologies have improved. Why has this not happened in the health care sector? Why is a CT scan or a pacemaker any different?

The answer is that the CT scan and the pacemaker are not fundamentally different in terms of their technological development, but that the pricing system for medical devices and services is radically different. While patients derive the primary benefits from treatments and products, insurance companies, government programs, and other third parties primarily pay for them. Once an insurance company or government program has approved payment for a particular procedure or product at a particular price, it is typically available to all similarly situated patients. As a result, the supplier obtains little or no competitive benefit from reducing prices. After the product or service (e.g., a particular type of pacemaker) is approved for use by the third-party payer at a particular price, the supplier has little prospect of increasing sales volume by reducing the price. As a result, technological improvements that reduce the cost of producing the pacemaker may not be passed along to patients or payers in the form of lower prices, but rather retained by the manufacturer in the form of higher profits.

Jason Fodeman and Robert A. Book,
"'Bending the Curve': What Really Drives
Health Care Spending," Wall Street Journal,
February 19, 2010. online.wsj.com.

residual increase should be attributed to technological change—what he calls "the enhanced capabilities of medicine."[7]

What Factors Affect the Growth of New Medical Technology?

Many factors influence innovation in medical care. Consumer demand for better health is a prime factor. Research shows that the use of medical care rises with income: as people and the nation become wealthier, they provide a fertile market for new medical innovations. Consumers want medical care that will help them achieve and maintain good health, and advances in medical technology are perceived as ways to promote those goals. Consumer demand is affected by the increased public awareness of medical technology through the media, the Internet, and direct-to-consumer advertising.

Health insurance systems that provide payment for new innovations also encourage medical advances. Medical treatments can be very expensive, and their cost would be beyond the reach of many people unless their risk of needing health care could be pooled though insurance (either public or private). The presence of health insurance provides some assurance to researchers and medical suppliers that patients will have the resources to pay for new medical products, thus encouraging research and development. At the same time, the promise of better health through improvements in medicine may increase the demand for health insurance by consumers looking for ways to assure access to the type of medical care that they want.

Health-Care Professionals Drive the Development of Medical Technology

The continuing flow of new medical technology results from other factors including the desire by professionals to find better ways to treat their patients and the level of investment in basic science and research. Direct providers of care may incorporate new technology because they want to improve the care they offer their patients, but they also may feel the need to offer the "latest and best" as they compete with other providers for patients. Health care professionals, like people in other occupations, also may be motivated by professional goals (e.g., peer recognition, tenure, prestige) to find ways to improve practice. Commercial interests (such as pharmaceutical companies and medical device makers) are willing to invest large amounts in research and development because they have found strong consumer interest in, and financial reimbursement for, many of the new products they produce. In addition, public and private investments in basic science research lead directly and indirectly to advancements in medical practice; these investments in basic science are not necessarily motivated by an interest in creating new products but by the desire to increase human understanding.

The United States Spends Billions on Health Research

An estimated $111 billion was spent on U.S. health research in 2005. The largest share was spent by Industry ($61 billion, or 55%), including the pharmaceutical industry ($35 billion, or 31%), the biotechnology industry ($16 billion, or 15%), and the medical technology industry ($10 billion, or 9%). Government spent $40 billion (36%), most of which was spent by the National Institutes of Health ($29 billion, or 26%), followed by other federal government agencies ($9 billion, or 8%), and state and local government ($3 billion, or 2%). Other Organizations (including universities, independent research institutes, voluntary health organizations, and philanthropic foundations) spent $10 billion (9%). About 5.5 cents of every health dollar was spent on health research in 2005, a decrease from 5.8 cents in 2004.[8] It is not known how much of health research was spent specifically on medical technology, though by definition most of the Industry spending ($61 billion) was spent on medical technology. Medical technology industries spent greater shares of research and development as a percent of sales in 2002 than did other U.S. industries:

11.4% for the Medical Devices industry and 12.9% for Drugs and Medicine, compared to 5.6% for Telecommunications, 4.1% for Auto, 3.9% for Electrical/Electronics, 3.5% for All Companies, and 3.1% for Aerospace/Defense.[9]

Greater Spending Does Not Equal Better Health Care

Rising health care expenditures lead to the question of whether we are getting value for the money we spend. Compared to other high-income countries, the U.S. spends more,[10] but this spending is not reflected in greater health care resources (such as hospital beds, physicians, nurses, MRIs, and CT scanners per capita)[11] or better measures of health.[12] However, studies have found that, on average, increases in medical spending as a result of advances in medical care have provided reasonable value. For example, [David M.] Cutler et al. found that from 1960 to 2000, average life expectancy increased by 7 years, 3.5 years of which they attribute to improvements in health care. Comparing the value of a year of life (anywhere from $50,000 to $200,000) to the study's finding that each year of increased life expectancy cost about $19,900 in health spending (after adjusting for inflation), the authors concluded that the increased spending, on average, has been worth it.[13]

No matter the value of advances in medical care, as the rapid growth in health care costs increasingly strains personal, corporate, and government budgets, policymakers and the public must consider the question of how much health care we can afford. Can the U.S. continue to spend an expanding share of GDP on health (from 7.2% in 1970 to a projected 20% by 2015)? If the answer is no, then society must consider ways to reduce future health spending growth. And since, as described earlier, the development and diffusion of new medical technology is a significant contributor to the rapid growth in health care spending, it is new technology that we would look to for cost savings.

Cost-Effectiveness Analysis Can Control Medical Technology Spending

Currently, most suggestions to slow the growth in new medical technology in the U.S. focus on cost-effectiveness analysis. Other approaches have problems: some used by other countries are not popular in the U.S. (rationing, regulation, budget-driven constraints), some have been tried and found not to have a significant impact on technology-driven costs (managed care, certificate-of-need approval), while others are expected to have only limited impact on health care spending (consumer-driven health care, pay-for-performance, information technology). Cost-effectiveness analysis involves non-biased, well-controlled studies of a technology's benefits and costs, followed by dissemination of the findings so they can be applied in clinical practice. The method to control the use of inappropriate technology could be through coverage and reimbursement decisions, by using financial incentives for physician and patients to use cost-effective treatments. Use of the cost-effectiveness findings could be implemented at the health plan level[14] or through a centralized, institutional process, such as Britain's National Institute for Health and Clinical Excellence (NICE). If implemented at the national level, questions about the structure, placement, financing, and function of a centralized agency would have to be resolved.[15] Other issues include whether money would be saved by reducing costly technology where marginal value is low and how to monitor the cost impact, and whether a cost containment approach would discourage technological innovation.

Notes

1. Centers for Medicare and Medicaid Services, Office of the Actuary, National Health Statistics Group, http://www.cms.hhs.gov/NationalHealthExpendData/ (see Historical, NHE summary including share of GDP, CY 1960-2005, file nhegdp05.zip; and Historical, Projected, NHE Historical and projections, 1965-2015, file nhe65-15.zip).
2. George B. Moseley III, *Changing Conditions for Medical Technology in the Health Care Industry* (presented before the OGI School of Science and Engineering, Oregon Health and Science University, October 18, 2005), http://cpd.ogi.edu/Seminars05/MoseleySeminarIndex.htm.

3. AdvaMed, *The Value of Investment in Health Care: Better Care, Better Lives* (January 2004): 14-21, at http://www.advamed.org/newsroom/medtap/medtapreport.pdf.

4. David M. Cutler and Mark McClellan, "Is Technological Change in Medicine Worth It?" *Health Affairs* 20(5) (September/October 2001): 11-29.

5. Richard A. Rettig, "Medical Innovation Duels Cost Containment," *Health Affairs* (Summer 1994): 15.

6. Several approaches have been used to study and quantify the impact of technology on health care costs, including:

   • The *residual approach*, where the impact of changes in other factors (such as prices, income, population growth and demographic changes, and utilization) is quantified, and the residual not accounted for is attributed to changes in technology. The most widely-used approach, it circumvents the need to specify a direct measure of technology and captures the impact of general technologies applied in the health sector, such as information technology. However, it is only a rough, indirect estimate (and perhaps an overestimate) of the impact of technology on health spending because other factors that cannot be quantified (such as lifestyle, environment, education) will also be included along with technology. Examples of residual studies include (1) Newhouse (1992), described in the text of this report; and (2) Edgar A. Peden and Mark S. Freeland, "Insurance Effects on US Medical Spending (1960-1993)," *Health Economics* 7 (1998): 671-687, which found that nearly half (47%) of the 1960-1993 growth in real per capita U.S. medical spending and almost two-thirds (64%) of its 1983-1993 growth were due to increasing levels of insurance coverage (i.e., a decline in coinsurance levels paid by consumers). Because lower coinsurance levels and higher research spending are considered inducers of technology, the authors concluded that these results imply that about two-thirds (70%) of the 1960-1993 medical spending growth and about three-fourths (76%) of the 1983-1993 medical spending growth came from cost-increasing advances in medical technology.

   • The *proxy approach*, where a proxy (such as research and development spending, or time) is used to measure the impact of technology. The usefulness of these studies depends on how good a substitute the proxy is for technology and how measurable it is. Examples include: (1) Albert A. Okunade and Vasudeva N.R. Murthy, "Technology as a "Major Driver" of Health Care Costs: a Cointegration Analysis of the Newhouse Conjecture," *Journal of Health Economics* 21 (2002): 147-159, which found that technological change, proxied by total research and development (R&D) spending and health R&D spending, is a statistically significant long-run driver of 1960-1997 rising real health care expenditures per capita; and (2) Livio Di Matteo, "The Macro Determinants of Health Expenditure in the United State and Canada: Assessing the Impact of Income, Age Distribution and Time," *Health Policy* 71(1) (January 2005): 23-42, which found that time, used as a proxy for technological change, accounted for about two-thirds of the 1975-2000 increases in real per capita health expenditures in the U.S. and Canada.

   • *Case studies of specific technologies*, to determine their effects on the cost of treating a particular condition. While case studies can explain the impact of certain medical advances on health care costs, it is difficult to generalize from them to an aggregate or national level: (1) In an analysis of technological change at the disease level for 5 medical conditions, David M. Cutler and Mark McClellan, "Is Technological Change In Medicine Worth It?" *Health Affairs* 20(5) (September/ October 2001): 11-29, found that the benefits of 4 of the 5 conditions studied (heart attacks, low-birthweight infants, depression, and cataracts) were greater than the costs; costs and benefits were about equal for the fifth condition (breast cancer). For example, in 1984 nearly 90% of heart attack patients were managed medically; by 1998, more than half of patients received surgical treatment. Spending by Medicare on heart attack patients increased from $3 billion to $4.8 billion (a 3.4% annual change), despite a 0.8% annual decline in the number of heart attacks. From 1984-1998, the use of new technology helped to increase the average heart attack patient's life expectancy by one year (valued at $70,000 per case), while treatment costs increased $10,000 per case (4.2% per year), for a net benefit of $60,000 per case; and (2) Laurence Baker et al., "The Relationship Between Technology Availability And Health Care Spending," *Health Affairs*, Web Exclusive (November 5, 2003): W3-537-W3-551, studied the relationship between the supply of new technologies and health care utilization and spending at 3 levels (a particular technology, "category" spending on substitutable or complimentary technologies, and total health spending), using 10 diagnostic imaging, cardiac, cancer, and newborn care technologies. They found that more availability of the technologies was frequently associated with higher use and spending on the services. For example, a one unit increase in the number of freestanding MRI units per million people was associated with an increase of about $32,900 per million beneficiaries (commercial and Medicare) per month, or approximately $395,000 per year. Looking at "category" spending, they found an individual technology can increase or decrease spending on other technologies in the same category depending on whether they complement those technologies (e.g., an increase of one unit per million in availability of MRI equipment was associated with an increase of 0.33% in total diagnostic imaging spending) or substitute for those technologies (e.g., increases in the availability of cardiac services were typically associated with reductions in total spending on patients with cardiac diagnoses). For total health care spending, they found that greater availability of technologies was associated with higher total spending in the commercial population in all but 2 technologies studied, and these effects were larger than the technology-specific relationships.

This endnote borrows heavily from (1) Mark S. Freeland, Stephen K. Heffler, and Sheila D. Smith, *The Impact of Technological Change on Health Care Cost Increases: A Brief Synthesis of the Literature*, June 1998, Office of the Actuary, Health Care Financing Administration; (2) Fabio Pammolli et al., *Medical Devices: Competitiveness and Impact on Public Health Expenditure* (July 2005), Center for the Economic Analysis of Competitiveness, Markets and Regulation (CERM), Rome, Italy; prepared for the Directorate Enterprise of the European Commission, http://ec.europa .eu/enterprise/medical_devices/c_f_f/md_final_report.pdf; and (3) Productivity Commission, Australian Government, *Impacts of Advances in Medical Technology in Australia*, August 31, 2005, Melbourne, Australia, http://www.pc.gov.au/study /medicaltechnology/finalreport/index.html.

7. Joseph P. Newhouse, "Medical Care Costs: How Much Welfare Loss?" *Journal of Economic Perspectives* 6(3) (Summer 1992): 3-21. For a thorough discussion of the components of health care spending growth and medical technology's significant role, see the report of the Technical Review Panel on the Medicare Trustees Reports, *Review of Assumptions and Methods of the Medicare Trustees' Financial Projections* (December 2000), http://www.cms.hhs.gov/ReportsTrustFunds /02_TechnicalPanelReports.asp#TopOfPage. The Panel concluded that estimates from

the literature suggest that about half of real health care expenditure growth has been attributable to medical technology (p. 35).

8. Research!America, *2005 Investment in U.S. Health Research*, September 2006, http://www.researchamerica.org/publications/appropriations/healthdollar2005.pdf. Data for the medical technology industry, universities, state and local government, and philanthropic foundations is for 2004.

9. AdvaMed, *The Medical Technology Industry at a Glance* (Sept. 7, 2004): 14, Chart 3.2, http://www.advamed.org/newsroom/chartbook.pdf.

10. Kaiser Family Foundation, *Health Care Spending in the United States and OECD Countries*, January 2007, http://www.kff.org/insurance/snapshot/chcm010307oth.cfm.

11. Gerard F. Anderson, Bianca K. Frogner, Roger A. Johns, and Uwe E. Reinhardt, "Health Care Spending And Use Of Information Technology In OECD Countries," *Health Affairs* 25(3) (May/June 2006): 819-831.

12. Cathy Schoen, Karen Davis, Sabrina K.H. How, and Stephen C. Schoenbaum, "U.S. Health System Performance: A National Scorecard," *Health Affairs*, Web Exclusive (September 20, 2006): w459.

13. David M. Cutler, Allison B. Rosen, and Sandeep Vijan, "The Value of Medical Spending in the United States, 1960-2000," *The New England Journal of Medicine*, 355(9) (August 31, 2006): 920-927. See also Jonathan S. Skinner, Douglas O. Staiger, and Elliott S. Fisher, "Is Technological Change In Medicine Always Worth It? The Case Of Acute Myocardial Infarction," *Health Affairs*, Web Exclusive (February 7, 2006): W34-W47, and Cutler and McClellan (2001).

14. Mark. V. Pauly, "Competition And New Technology," *Health Affairs* 24(6) (November/December 2005): 1523-1535.

15. Gail R. Wilensky, "Developing A Center For Comparative Effectiveness Information," *Health Affairs*, Web Exclusive (November 7, 2006): w572-w585; Molly Joel Coye and Jason Kell, "How Hospitals Confront New Technology," *Health Affairs* 25(1) (Januaryl/February 2006): 163-173; and the NICE website: http://www.nice.org.uk/page.aspx?o=home.

"States with larger increases in the
quality of diagnostic procedures,
drugs, and physicians . . . did not have
larger increases in per capita medical
expenditure."

New Technology Does Not Increase the Cost of Health Care

Frank R. Lichtenberg

In the following viewpoint, an economic researcher refutes claims that new medical technology is contributing to the rise of health-care costs. In his own study on how quality care and behavioral risk factors affect life expectancy, he finds that there is a lack of correlation between medical innovation and expenditure growth when comparing data across states, and, in fact, increased health insurance coverage is correlated with lower medical expense. Frank R. Lichtenberg is a professor at Columbia University's Graduate School of Business and a research associate at the National Bureau of Economic Research.

As you read, consider the following questions:

1. What three measures of quality care did Lichtenberg identify for his study?

2. What was the change in life expectancy between 1991 and 2004, according to the author?

3. What amount of change in life expectancy is unexplained by Lichtenberg's data?

The cost of medical care continues to rise rapidly in the US and other industrialised countries. According to a report from consulting firm PricewaterhouseCoopers, US employers who offer health insurance coverage could see a 9% cost increase between 2009 and 2010, and their workers may face an even larger increase.

Some observers argue that rapidly increasing health care expenditure is due, to an important extent, to medical innovation —the development and use of new drugs, diagnostics, and procedures. For example, the Kaiser Family Foundation, citing [Richard A.] Rettig, claims that "advances in medical technology have contributed to rising overall US health care spending."

Other observers argue that most medical innovations do not improve people's health. Lexchin, for example, claims that "at best one third of new drugs offer some additional clinical benefit and perhaps as few as 3% are major therapeutic advances."

New Findings Indicate Innovation Does Not Increase Medical Expense

If both of these claims were true, medical innovation would result in the worst of both worlds—a large increase in cost and little or no increase in benefit (in the form of improved health outcomes). However, a study that I have recently performed casts considerable doubt on both of these claims. My findings indicate that medical innovation has yielded significant increases in life expectancy without increasing medical expenditure.

My study examines the effect of the quality of medical care, behavioural risk factors, and other variables on life expectancy and medical expenditure using longitudinal state-level data. . . .

The rate of increase of longevity has varied considerably across US states since 1991.

I examined the effects of three different measures of the quality of medical care. The first is the average quality of diagnostic imaging procedures, defined as the fraction of procedures that are advanced procedures. The second is the mean vintage (FDA approval year) of outpatient and inpatient prescription drugs. The third is the average quality of practicing physicians, defined as the fraction of physicians that were trained at top-ranked medical schools.

I also examined the effects on longevity of three important behavioural risk factors—obesity, smoking, and AIDS incidence—and other variables—education, income, and health insurance coverage—that might be expected to influence longevity growth. My econometric approach controlled for the effects of unobserved factors that vary across states but are relatively stable over time (e.g. climate and environmental quality), and unobserved factors that change over time but are invariant across states (e.g. changes in federal government policies).

Medical Innovation Improves Life Expectancy

The indicators of the quality of diagnostic imaging procedures, drugs, and physicians almost always had positive and statistically significant effects on life expectancy. Life expectancy increased more rapidly in states where (1) the fraction of Medicare diagnostic imaging procedures that were advanced procedures increased more rapidly, (2) the vintage of self- and provider-administered drugs increased more rapidly, and (3) the quality of medical schools previously attended by physicians increased more rapidly.

Between 1991 and 2004, life expectancy at birth increased 2.37 years. The estimates imply that, during this period, the increased use of advanced imaging technology increased life expectancy by 0.62–0.71 years, use of newer outpatient prescription drugs increased life expectancy by 0.96–1.26 years, and use of newer provider-administered drugs increased life expectancy by 0.48–0.54 years. The decline in the average quality of medical schools previously attended by physicians reduced life expectancy by 0.28–0.47 years.

Mortality Rates in Australia Are Comparable to the United States

The availability of data from Australia's universal health care system, Medicare Australia, allowed me to provide some additional evidence about the impact of advanced imaging technology on mortality. I estimated difference-in-difference models of the effect of advanced imaging innovation on age-specific mortality rates. Demographic groups that had above-average increases in the number of advanced imaging procedures per capita had above-average declines in mortality rates, but changes in mortality rates were uncorrelated across demographic groups with changes in the number of standard imaging procedures per capita. Estimates of the effect of diagnostic imaging innovation on longevity based on Australian data are quite consistent with estimates based on US data.

The increased fraction of the population that was overweight or obese, rising from 44% to 59%, reduced the increase in life expectancy by .58–.68 years. The decline in the incidence of AIDS is estimated to have increased life expectancy by .18–.20 years. The small decline in smoking prevalence may have increased life expectancy by about 0.10 years.

Growth in life expectancy was uncorrelated across states with health insurance coverage and education, and inversely correlated with per capita income growth. The 19% increase in real per capita income is estimated to have reduced life expectancy by .34–.43 years. The sum of the contributions of all of the factors to the increase in life expectancy is in the 0.85–1.32 year range. Consequently, between 1.05 and 1.52 years of the 2.37-year increase in life expectancy is unexplained.

New Medical Technology Has Led to
Greater Coverage and Lower Costs

Although states with larger increases in the quality of diagnostic procedures drugs, and physicians had larger increases in life expectancy, they did not have larger increases in per capita medical expenditure. This may be the case because, while newer diagnostic procedures and drugs are more expensive than their older counterparts, they may reduce the need for costly additional medical treatment. The absence of a correlation across states between medical innovation and expenditure growth is inconsistent with the view that advances in medical technology have contributed to rising overall US health care spending. Increased health insurance coverage is associated with lower growth in per capita medical expenditure.

> "Medicare recipients are receiving
> certain kinds of surgeries more
> frequently and are admitted for longer
> periods to intensive care units during
> their final days."

Medical Technology Adds to Medicare Costs

Jordan Rau

In the following viewpoint, a journalist argues that the cost of Medicare is increasing because of new medical procedures. Compensation in the health-care industry favors specialists, potentially leading, he contends, to unnecessary tests and procedures being performed to justify the high cost of equipment. Jordan Rau is a Kaiser Health News *reporter.*

As you read, consider the following questions:

1. According to the author, what is the percentage increase of Medicare spending in the Provo, Utah, region as compared to the rest of the United States from 2000 to 2007?

Jordan Rau, "Medical Spending Spiking in Once Thrifty Areas," *Kaiser Health News*, March 10, 2010; adapted by the author(s). Kaiser Health News is an editorially independent program of the Henry J. Kaiser Family Foundation, a nonprofit, nonpartisan health policy research and communication organization not affiliated with Kaiser Permanente. This information was reprinted with permission from the Henry J. Kaiser Family Foundation. The Kaiser Family Foundation, a leader in health policy analysis, health journalism and communication, is dedicated to filling the need for trusted, independent information on the major health issues facing our nation and its people. The Foundation is a non-profit private operating foundation, based in Menlo Park, California.

2. What is the percentage increase of procedures performed on Medicare patients from 2000 to 2008, as described by Rau?

3. In the viewpoint, what medical procedure does Greg Poulson find frustrating because its benefit does not outweigh its cost?

If there is any place that should have medical spending under control, this [Provo, Utah] is it.

Residents are among the healthiest in the country. Many are Mormons who don't smoke or drink, and outdoorsy folks devoted to active lives. The biggest hospital is run by Intermountain Healthcare, a medical system lauded by President Barack Obama for providing high quality care while restraining costs.

Until recently, Provo seemed to be a model for the nation. But spending on Medicare patients here has accelerated rapidly, as it has in many other areas of the country also known for cost-efficient care. The region's transformation calls into question initiatives—including some in the new health care law [the 2010 Patient Protection and Affordable Care Act]—to encourage more profligate regions to learn from their frugal counterparts.

A major reason: Medicare recipients are receiving certain kinds of surgeries more frequently and are admitted for longer periods to intensive care units during their final days.

"It's very discouraging to see costs increasing rapidly in those low-cost areas we believe to have good care," says Paul Ginsburg, president of the Center for Studying Health System Change, a Washington-based research group. "They appear to be succumbing to the same forces that have led to high costs elsewhere."

Experts say Medicare spending trends often parallel those in the country's overall health system. In 2007, average Medicare spending per person in the greater Provo hospital market was

$8,064. That was below the national average of $8,682, but far higher than it had been a few years before.

Between 2000 and 2007, Medicare spending in the Provo region rose on average 8.6 percent a year, nearly double the average national rate of 4.7 percent, according to data from the Dartmouth Atlas of Health Care, which analyzes geographic variations in health spending.

Medicare Spending Rises

Provo's spending increases aren't an aberration. Annual average spending grew at 7 percent or more in other traditionally low-cost areas, including Oxford, Miss.; Wausau, Wis.; and Durham, N.C. Even in Rochester, Minn., home of the highly regarded Mayo Clinic, and Salt Lake City, where Intermountain is headquartered, Medicare costs grew faster than the national average, according to Dartmouth.

On their own, these areas aren't big enough to bankrupt Medicare. Still, the spending increases are particularly worrisome in places such as Provo where many providers have already made changes experts hope can hold down costs. These include adopting electronic medical records, focusing on prevention and increasing cooperation between doctors and hospitals.

But Harvard professor Michael Chernew noted in a recent [2010] article that "even the most efficient delivery systems must wrestle with the adoption of expensive new technologies." Indeed, Provo's regional hospital market, which stretches south of Salt Lake City down the Wasatch mountain range and includes more than 26,000 Medicare beneficiaries, has embraced some of the less admired traits of expensive health care markets, with dueling providers competing to offer the same kinds of high-tech services.

"The first surgical center in Utah County was built by a physician from the hospital," says Rulon Barlow, a former county health board commissioner who runs the student health center at Brigham Young University in Provo. "So what did the hospital do? It built a surgery center. It wasn't too much longer that another outfit came in across the street."

Doctors Who Offer More Services Earn More Money

Much of this kind of rapid expansion is fueled by the Medicare's traditional fee-for-service payment system, which rewards doctors who offer more services, health care experts say. Patients, for their part, seem only too happy to get the latest that medical technology has to offer, as close to home as possible. Physicians in the Provo region performed 17.3 percent more procedures on Medicare patients in 2008 than they did in 2000, outpacing the median national increase of 13.7 percent, according to a Government Accountability Office study.

The largest physician-owned practice in the state is the Provo-based Central Utah Clinic, which has grown fivefold over the decade and now houses more than 110 doctors, mostly specialists. Last year, it earned gross revenues of $200 million, clinic administrator Scott Barlow says, and its doctors saw 208,000 patients. That's a remarkable number given that only 556,000 people reside in the Provo-Orem metropolitan area.

Central Utah Clinic's sprawling campus, which sits across the street from Intermountain's Utah Valley Regional Medical Center, has opened its own open heart program, chemotherapy center and a high-dose radiation machine so powerful that it operates behind 70,000 pound steel doors in a room called "the vault." The clinic is home to some of the only providers in the area in a number of specialties, including cardiology.

Some Doctors Avoid Unnecessary Procedures

The physicians have attempted to make it a one-stop shop for patients, even building a pharmacy on the lot. The physician-owners benefit financially from the use of these machines and facilities (except the pharmacy, which Utah law prohibits them from owning), but the clinic's officials insist they guard carefully against performing unneeded procedures.

Dr. Scott Bingham, a cardiologist at the Central Utah Clinic, says area cardiologists have been performing fewer of the most expensive tests and surgeries in the last few years, which Dartmouth has not yet analyzed. "The only thing that I see increasing in Provo is the number of patients we see," he says.

Competitors are skeptical. "The gastroenterologists owning their own CT scanners, the oncologists owning their own radiation machines," says Dr. Wendell Gibby, a radiologist who owns his own imaging clinic. "If you've got a million dollar scanner, you end up using it," he says.

Intermountain also faces competition from HCA, the for-profit hospital chain. In 1998, HCA, welcomed into the area by commercial insurers feeling captive to paying whatever Intermountain charged, built Timpanogos Regional Hospital in Orem, the city just north of Provo. HCA also owns a hospital in the south. Timpanogos opened its own heart surgery program in 2007, and last year added two stories on top of the existing two floors.

Dr. Mike Kennedy, a family doctor and the chief of staff at Timpanogos, speculates that the area's higher Medicare costs are due to better care. "You're probably seeing more aggressive treatment earlier on in disease stages," he says. "If we want excellent care, it's going to cost excellent money."

Marketing and Consumer Demand Drive New Medical Technology

To some, it's inevitable [that] low cost areas such as Provo will catch up to their more expensive peers as a greater proportion of medical spending goes toward expensive machines and nursing salaries, which are rising, says Greg Poulson, senior vice president at Intermountain. Aggressive marketing of the latest technology also is making it more likely that patients everywhere are demanding the same novel treatments, even ones that aren't proven to work better, Poulson says.

"We're seeing a homogenization of practice," Poulson says. He says "at Intermountain we're trying not to cave into things that we think are value diminishing. An example that I find frustrating is the use of robotics for surgery."

Yet Intermountain has embraced the technology, too, announcing in 2008 that its surgeons in Salt Lake City "performed the first robotic surgery using the most advanced robotic surgical system in the world that utilizes 3-D technology and high definition (HD) vision that virtually extends the surgeon's eyes and hands deep into the surgical field." Utah Valley Regional has been busy growing in many areas. It's added four MRI machines; expanded its intensive and critical care units; upgraded its trauma center; doubled the size of its emergency room; and built an outpatient center.

Treatments for Medicare Patients Are on the Rise

Amid all this new construction, Medicare patients in the region have been getting more and more medical attention. Dartmouth data covering 2000 through 2005 show some treatments were performed more frequently in Provo while decreasing nationally. Those included operations to clear blocked leg arteries and replace heart valves. Repairs of aortic aneurisms and hospitalizations for hypertension and asthma also rose faster than the national average. While many procedures are still performed less frequently than elsewhere, a Dartmouth study released in April singled out Provo for having the highest shoulder replacement rate in the country.

Commercial insurers say prices in Provo and the rest of Utah still remain lower than the national average. But some experts say that could change, too.

"We take some comfort that we have less of [a] problem in Utah than elsewhere," says Dr. Kim Bateman, vice president for medical affairs at HealthInsight, a Salt Lake City-based nonprofit that Medicare has authorized to find ways to improve the quality of care in Utah and Nevada. "But really I think we're just behind them on the same curve—that we're going to be subject to the same kinds of cost pressures as everyone else."

> *"Medicare coverage determinations can act as a policy lever to influence . . . the appropriate use of medical technology."*

Better Regulation of Medical Technology Can Contain Medicare Costs

Sean R. Tunis, Robert A. Berenson, Steve E. Phurrough, and Penny E. Mohr

In the following viewpoint, researchers examine the problems Medicare has with coverage and payments, especially regarding the use of new technology. According to the authors, the Centers for Medicare and Medicaid Services (CMS) has largely been unable to pursue its own research into what technology is appropriate and cost-effective for its patients. The authors maintain that CMS should conduct more national coverage reviews of new medical technology in order to provide better care to patients and keep costs down. Sean R. Tunis, Steve E. Phurrough, and Penny E. Mohr work for the Center for Medical Technology Policy, based in Baltimore, Maryland. Robert A. Berenson works for the Urban Institute in Washington, DC.

Sean R. Tunis, Robert A. Berenson, Steve E. Phurrough, and Penny E. Mohr, "Introduction" and "Discussions and Recommendations," *Improving the Quality and Efficiency of the Medicare Program Through Coverage Policy*, August 2011, pp. 1–2, 12–14. Copyright © 2011 by the Urban Institute. All rights reserved. Reproduced by permission.

As you read, consider the following questions:

1. According to the authors, what is the Triple Aim of the Medicare program?

2. What changes would CMS have to make to become more active in reviewing new technologies, according to the authors?

3. What three statutory changes do the authors of the viewpoint propose in order to strengthen the Medicare program?

In the face of large and growing budget deficits, finding ways to bend the health care cost curve and improve the efficiency of the Medicare program has been a central focus of budget policy. Medicare spends more than $500 billion annually for more than 46 million senior and disabled beneficiaries, and research suggests new medical technologies such as drugs, devices, diagnostics and surgical techniques are a major driver of increasing costs. For example, some novel anti-cancer drugs now cost significantly more than older alternatives, many new diagnostic technologies are additive rather than replacing outmoded or older services, and advances in minimally invasive surgical techniques have substantially expanded the number of people who are now surgical candidates. Within the fee-for-service environment, which makes up the vast majority of Medicare spending, there are few incentives to be efficient or economical. While some advances in medicine undoubtedly have contributed to reductions in morbidity and mortality, new technology and new uses of established technology are often adopted with little evidence that they work better than existing treatments. There is even less evidence about which patients might actually be harmed by their use.

Coverage policy examines the clinical evidence to decide which services and treatments should be paid for by insurance and under what circumstances. Medicare coverage determinations can act as a policy lever to influence both the appropriate use of medical technology and the creation of better evidence to support clinical and health policy decisions.

How Medicare Processes Claims

Currently, Medicare defers most coverage decisions to regional contractors who process claims on a daily basis. The emphasis of these contractors' work is on efficiently processing claims rather than accurately evaluating clinical effectiveness or appropriateness of the services provided. There is also a dearth of information available to the contractors about the details of these services, leading to missed opportunities to prevent ineffective, unproven and/or harmful technologies from widespread adoption, at a significant cost to the program. Even when national policies are developed, the Centers for Medicare and Medicaid Services (CMS) and the administrative contractors often lack the resources to assure that the policies are implemented as written. Dependent on research performed by other agencies, CMS often must make coverage policy decisions while lacking high-priority, clinical research relevant to the Medicare population. In essence, CMS is precluded from taking action to restrict the coverage of services that do not provide added value to patients when compared to available alternatives that are sometimes less expensive.

Medicare Needs to Revise Coverage and Payment Policies Regarding New Technology

The four authors of this [viewpoint] have each been senior officials at CMS with direct responsibility for core aspects of coverage and payment policy. The observations presented here reflect our consensus viewpoint on how things now work at CMS and how they might be altered. We support our observations and recommendations with evidence and opinion provided by other experts in this field.

This [viewpoint's] premise is that the process for making coverage decisions in Medicare falls short of its potential to contribute to the recently articulated "Triple Aim" of the program to (1) improve the individual experience of care, (2) improve the health of populations, and (3) reduce per capita costs of care for populations. Most Triple Aim attention has been focused on how organizations providing health services can be encouraged to become Triple Aim "integrators" on behalf of the populations they serve. That is the role of accountable care organizations, as envisioned by the Patient Protection and Affordable Care Act (ACA). However, payers can also play a decisive role in promoting Triple Aim objectives. While a broad policy audience may consider policy about coverage and payment of technology a technical aspect of program administration with little direct relevance to beneficiary well-being and the financial status of the Medicare program, the authors argue that Medicare coverage and payment policies for new technology represent a fertile mechanism through which to achieve the Triple Aim. . . .

Medicare Coverage Policy Can Be Repaired

This [viewpoint] concludes with high-priority recommendations for reform. Some changes could be relatively easy to implement with sufficient leadership, political will and adequate administrative resources. Other changes would require more significant and politically difficult actions dependent on affirmative congressional authority that does not now exist. These more ambitious recommendations are made anticipating that any fundamental reconsideration and possible restructuring of the Medicare program should thoroughly review the current limitations in the CMS coverage process.

This [viewpoint] does not explore all aspects of Medicare's potential to influence the use of technologies. For example, many believe that patients should be more fully engaged than they are currently with their health professionals in shared decision-making about when and how to apply available technology in their particular circumstances. Approaches to achieving shared decision-making, such as with accountable care organizations and patient-centered medical homes, are beyond the scope of this [viewpoint]. Nor does it explore provider payment incentives, which surely affect the use and the costs associated with technology. The decision on whether to employ an available technology is an inherently different decision than determining whether the technology should be made available and paid for by the program and whether any restrictions should be placed on that coverage. The focus of this [viewpoint] is the process of making coverage policies, not Medicare's influence on health professionals and their patients' decisions to use covered items and services. . . .

Medicare Coverage Policy Is Uneven

CMS has recently emphasized its programmatic Triple Aim as improving patients' experience of care, improving the health of a population and slowing the rise in per capita costs—an approach that reflects similar objectives inherent in the concept of value-based purchasing. Value-based purchasing emphasizes the desire to obtain higher quality with more prudent and, likely, lower spending.

To support value-based purchasing, Congress and CMS have emphasized measurement of provider performance and have begun to modify payment approaches to better align payment with demonstrated provider quality and efficiency. However, the leading cause of increased health spending—adoption of new technology and increased use of existing technology—has not been a prominent focus of value-based purchasing initiatives, nor has there been any recent movement by Medicare to directly address the health effects or costs associated with the use of new technologies. In fact, Congress has occasionally challenged attempts by CMS to make coverage decisions based on a careful appraisal of available scientific evidence from peer-reviewed clinical journals, creating a very cautious environment at CMS. Further, CMS and its regional administrative contractors lack sufficient resources and will to appropriately implement the coverage decisions they do make.

As a result, some items and services that do not benefit Medicare patients are provided, often at high cost to the program, while other services that would improve patient health and well-being are underused, with no clear incentives to promote their adoption. The implication is that addressing some of the current programmatic deficiencies in coverage policy could improve care while reducing program spending.

Attempts to Control Medicare Spending Are Controversial

ACA established the controversial Independent Payment Advisory Board (IPAB) to hold Medicare spending within legislated limits, with Congress required to either accept the board's proposals or come up with alternatives that achieve similar savings. If no legislative action is taken, the IPAB's recommendations would take effect. Because of its specific legislative charter, policy analysts expect IPAB to focus mostly on payment rates and payment methods, not coverage policies and procedures. IPAB is specifically prohibited from making recommendations that would result in "rationing" of care, although the term is not defined in statute, and is also prohibited from making recommendations that would limit benefits. Some opponents of IPAB would surely argue that changes in how Medicare considers approval for coverage of new technology at least constitutes limiting benefits, if not overt rationing. In short, it is unlikely that IPAB, even if it survives current political efforts to prevent its creation, will play a significant role in supporting a stronger coverage process at CMS and the administrative contractors.

Nevertheless, Medicare's recent commitment to improving the patient experience of care and health outcomes at lower per capita cost could be more effectively supported through Medicare coverage policy by considering the following recommendations. These are organized based on their potential ability to improve the Medicare program and by the practical feasibility of adoption.

Improvements to the Current Medicare Coverage Policy Approach Are Needed

CMS has become increasingly reluctant to use its existing "reasonable and necessary" statutory authority to make or modify national coverage decisions even when based on very high-quality evidence. The agency should seriously explore the policy and legal concerns behind this trend. As discussed earlier, even when the agency had strong scientific evidence that casts doubt on the effectiveness of a technology or service to improve patient health and well-being, it did not move forward, partly because of a political environment that makes such evidence-based policy-making a target for affected stakeholders.

The MEDCAC [Medicare Evidence Development and Coverage Advisory Committee] could help CMS craft a more systematic approach to identifying topics for review as national coverage determinations. For CMS to become more active in reviewing technologies, it would be necessary to augment the size and expertise of the staff that conducts clinical and scientific reviews, most of whom are housed in the Coverage and Analysis Group. Additional resources would also be important to permit the agency and its contractors to monitor compliance with the clinical conditions described in local and national coverage decisions.

Selective use of prior authorization for high-cost items with demonstrated inappropriate use should also be considered as a way to improve adherence to evidence-based coverage conditions. If the additional resources were provided with accountability for their use, it is likely that the increased administrative costs would be more than offset with program savings resulting from reduction of services that do not benefit—or actually harm—Medicare beneficiaries.

Shifting Policy Focus from a Biomedical Perspective to Relevant Outcomes

Health care policymakers have long called on payers to shift from a narrow biomedical perspective—which considers a technology's safety and efficacy in terms of intermediate or short-term end points—to a wider perspective that considers whether technology improves final outcomes of interest—such as functional status, quality of life, disability, major clinical events, and death—and whether it does so in typical patient populations.

Peter J. Newmann and Sean R. Tunis,
"Medicare and Medical Technology—The
Growing Demand for Relevant Outcomes,"
New England Journal of Medicine, *vol. 362,*
2010, pp. 377–379.

Medicare Should Conduct More National Coverage Reviews for New Technology

Medicare could also use its existing coverage authority to more actively conduct national coverage reviews of new technologies that are likely to provide important health benefits for Medicare beneficiaries. While CMS took this approach with national coverage of smoking cessation therapy, there have been few other examples to date of specific high-value technologies being promoted through the coverage process, and no current policy strategy or mechanism exists to pursue this approach.

CMS should expand the use of national coverage decisions to actively promote adoption of high-value technologies that are underused, including interventions that may help reduce the need for costly subsequent interventions. CMS should seek opportunities to promote delivery system innovations that will be tested through the Center for Medicare and Medicaid Innovations that could be facilitated through NCDs [national coverage determinations] on individual items and services that might be included in those demonstration programs.

With the advice of the MEDCAC, CMS could identify important needs and current gaps in services in the Medicare program to better support care for elderly and disabled beneficiaries, sending clear signals to product developers and providers about high-impact areas for investment to develop new products and services.

It would also be worth conducting a more careful review of the regional and local coverage process in order to identify how this critical aspect of Medicare coverage policy is conducted. Given the significant impact of these decisions and the uptake of new health care technologies, the effect of any proposed changes in national coverage policy will depend in part on a robust, consistent and evidence-based regional process with sufficient resources to monitor provider compliance.

Medicare Needs to Identify and Promote Its Research Priorities

Medicare's ability to develop evidence-based coverage policy is severely restricted by its relatively limited capacity to ensure that its research priorities are weighed seriously in the allocation of public research funds. CMS has no budget to support clinical research. Additionally, the major public funders of research have little interest in ensuring that Medicare's programmatic needs are significant factors in the scientific review process.

CMS could make more deliberate use of the MEDCAC to help identify critical research priorities and then provide these recommendations to NIH [National Institutes of Health], AHRQ [Agency for Healthcare Research and Quality], PCORI

[Patient-Centered Outcomes Research Institute] and private-sector research funders for consideration. Agencies within the federal government, including NIH in particular, should be more attentive to the practical needs of CMS for comparative effectiveness research relevant to the Medicare program. In addition to developing a process to articulate these research priorities, it will be necessary to establish HHS [Department of Health and Human Services] policies or other policy mechanisms to ensure that at least some CMS clinical research questions are given higher priority. Otherwise, the poor quality of evidence currently hampering Medicare's ability to make evidence-based clinical policy will continue.

New Statutory Authorities Would Strengthen Medicare

Three specific statutory changes would contribute significantly to Medicare's ability to use the coverage process more effectively.

First, it would be useful to establish explicit legal authority that would allow CMS to apply "coverage with evidence development" to promising technologies that are particularly important to Medicare beneficiaries and require better evidence to answer important questions about their clinical effectiveness. The current authority is sufficiently ambiguous to prevent CMS from fully developing and implementing coverage with evidence development consistently and systematically. The historical difficulty in addressing coverage policy through legislation and regulation suggests that statutory refinements will be challenging, though clearly critical to achieving essential programmatic goals.

Second, Congress should restore and expand Medicare's authority to apply LCA [least costly alternative] pricing to products that are similar in their biological and/or physical characteristics and that achieve comparable clinical outcomes.

Finally, statutory changes will be necessary to allow Medicare to explicitly consider costs as part of the national coverage process. This will almost certainly require explicit statutory authority, given the clear evidence that past efforts to accomplish this through regulatory action have been stymied. Consideration of costs should not be based on the formal cost-effectiveness analysis as embodied in QALY [quality-adjusted life year] calculations. Instead, CMS should be allowed to deny coverage and/ or reduce the pricing for technologies that provide health outcomes comparable to already covered, but less costly, technologies. More difficult to address will be technologies that provide small incremental benefits at significantly higher prices. In such cases, Congress may need to consider new pricing authorities for Medicare that allow CMS to link prices to incremental benefits. This approach will be necessary until payment reforms have been successfully implemented that create financial incentives for providers and/or patients to have some sensitivity to the relative benefits and costs of the technologies being used.

The Future of Medicare

As the Medicare program enters a new phase of rapid evolution following the passage of ACA, many new programs, demonstrations, pilots and policies are being pursued, all of which aim to improve the individual experience of care, improve the health of populations and reduce per capita costs of care. There is substantial room to improve the implementation of existing policy processes to achieve these aims, particularly with respect to Medicare coverage policy. Much can be achieved by more deliberate use of existing authorities and procedures, and further substantial gains would result from ACA's additional clarifications of CMS's authority. Although the main focus of Medicare reform has been to shift Medicare away from the underlying fee-for-service payment approach, significant benefits to the program and Medicare beneficiaries could also result from the improvements in CMS's activities in determining and implementing coverage of services that are recommended in this [viewpoint].

> "The impending medical device tax
> . . . will boost the nation's medical bills
> while causing the loss of high-paying
> manufacturing jobs."

The Medical Device Tax Will Devastate the Medical Technology Industry

Devon Herrick

In the following viewpoint, a researcher discusses the possible detrimental effects of the 2.3 percent tax on wholesale medical devices scheduled to go into effect in 2013. He contends that the tax will force smaller medical companies to become even smaller to absorb the loss of income and, ultimately, this will lead to job losses and higher medical bills. Devon Herrick is a senior fellow with the National Center for Policy Analysis.

As you read, consider the following questions:

1. According to Herrick, how much was paid in corporate taxes by medical device firms in 2006?
2. How many people are employed in the US medical device industry, as reported by Herrick?

Devon Herrick, "The Job-Killing Medical Device Tax," National Center for Policy Analysis Issue Brief No. 106, February 15, 2012, Copyright © 2012 by the National Center for Policy Analysis. All rights reserved. Reproduced by permission.

3. What is the estimated number of jobs lost due to the medical device tax, according to the viewpoint?

Americans consume nearly $100 billion dollars worth of medical devices annually. Medical devices include simple things, such as cotton swabs, as well as complex instruments, such as pacemakers and artificial joints.

In 2010, Congress passed a tax on medical devices to off-set a portion of the $1 trillion cost of the Patient Protection and Affordable Care Act (ACA). Beginning in 2013, a 2.3 percent tax will be imposed on the manufacture and importation of medical devices. Devices typically sold by retailers to consumers—including toothbrushes and bandages—are exempt from the tax, whereas devices purchased from wholesalers by health care providers, such as tongue depressors and ultrasound equipment, will be taxed.

Though seemingly small, if this tax is implemented it will destroy jobs and stifle innovation.

What Is a Medical Device?

A medical device can be "an instrument, apparatus, implement, machine, contrivance, implant, in vitro reagent, or other similar or related article, including a component part," according to the U.S. Food and Drug Administration (FDA).

Medical devices fall into one of three regulatory classes based on the level of risk they pose to patients:

- Class I devices have the least risk and thus require the least regulatory control; indeed, most of the items found in local pharmacies are Class I medical devices.

- Class II devices are more closely scrutinized by the FDA and include such things as patient monitors, diagnostic imaging machines and laboratory equipment.

- Class III medical devices—the most highly regulated—include life-sustaining devices, such as pacemakers and drug-coated arterial stents, as well as orthopedic implants, such as artificial hips and knees.

The Impact of the Medical Device Tax

The 2.3 percent tax will be imposed on revenue, not profits. This means the tax will be paid even on devices sold at a loss. Further, the increased tax burden represents a significant portion of the profit margin on each dollar of medical device sales:

- In 2006 the medical device industry paid corporate income taxes of $3.1 billion on taxable income of $13.7 billion.
- The medical device tax would add approximately $3 billion annually to the taxes paid by medical device firms—a 100 percent increase.

Medical device firms in the United States are relatively small—about 95 percent have annual sales of less than $100 million. Over the 2013 to 2019 period, these firms would pay a projected $20 billion in additional taxes—imposing one of the highest effective corporate tax rates in the world.

The Effect of a Medical Device Tax on the Industry

How firms respond to the new tax will vary. To the extent they can, medical device makers will have an incentive to raise prices across the board to cover the cost of the tax. Although the industry is highly competitive, the fact that the tax applies to all firms could easily prompt industry-wide price increases.

Characteristics, profit margins and business practices vary within each segment of the industry, but those firms with relatively high profit margins will likely fare better than firms with thin margins. Thus, the tax will impact some firms more than others. For instance, device maker Zoll could see its profits fall by 40 percent, whereas Abiomed would see its losses pushed further into the red by 19 percent. . . .

The Medical Device Tax Will Raise Prices for End Users

The new excise tax is complex, and it will substantially raise the tax burden on the medical device manufacturing industry. In response to the new tax, prices of medical devices will rise, and consumers and health care providers will pay more for medical devices. The exact change in prices for medical devices as a result of the excise tax will depend on various economic parameters, but an estimated half or more of the excise tax will likely be passed along to end users in terms of higher prices. Correspondingly, the quantity of medical devices demanded will decline in response to the higher prices that include the excise taxes.

Diana Furchtgott-Roth and Harold Furchtgott-Roth, Employment Effects of the New Excise Tax on the Medical Device Industry, *Advanced Medical Technology Association, September 2011.*

Medical device makers have already been adversely affected by the downturn in the economy, as patients postpone elective procedures like hip and knee replacements due to cost-sharing requirements. In addition, the recession has produced a more risk-averse investment environment, prompting more medical device firms to turn to Europe for then new product launches. Indeed, a Northwestern University study found that about three-fourths of medical device makers initially launch new products overseas, where device approval takes less time and the regulatory environment is more predictable.

Changes in profitability for U.S.-based operations could ultimately encourage producers to look for lower-cost options abroad. Moving more of the industry offshore could potentially result in supply disruptions or shortages of certain devices.

The Effect of a Medical Device Tax on Workers

The U.S. medical device industry employs more than 423,000 workers across the United States, who collectively earn about $25 billion annually. According to the Lewin Group, a consulting firm that studies the impact of public policy, workers in this sector earn an average of $58,188 per year—about 40 percent more than average U.S. pay. In many states the medical device industry pays a wage premium of nearly 50 percent or more compared to the average wage.

High-paying middle class jobs benefit local economies as well as the individuals who receive the paychecks. Communities benefit from the demand for other goods and services these positions create. For example, the state median job multiplier in the medical device industry is 2.5, meaning for every one job in the medical device industry an additional 1.5 jobs are indirectly created to provide additional services such as housing and groceries.

The medical device tax will result in the loss of high-paying manufacturing jobs. Indeed, firms have already begun preparing for the tax by reducing payrolls:

- In November 2011, device maker Stryker Corporation announced its intention to lay off 1,000 workers in order to cut costs in advance of the tax.

- Another firm, Covidien Plc, announced the layoff of 200 U.S. workers and plans to offshore production to Mexico and Costa Rica.

- The tax will prompt the loss of about 45,661 jobs across the medical device industry, according to Diana Furchtgott-Roth, former chief Labor Department economist.

The Effect of the Medical Device Tax on Health-Care Costs

The medical device tax will ultimately increase national health expenditures, according to the Office of the Actuary for the Centers for Medicare and Medicaid Services. Health care providers, hospitals, doctors and patients, as well as insurers, will bear much of the additional cost of the tax. To the extent that device makers are unable to pass on their additional costs, innovation and medical device workers will suffer.

Congress would be wise to repeal the impending medical device tax. It is a blow to an industry that provides goods essential to the health of Americans. The tax will boost the nation's medical bills while causing the loss of high-paying manufacturing jobs, and the potential tax revenue is relatively small compared to the costs.

> *"Economic research shows that health-related spending is relatively inelastic: When prices go up, demand falls by only a fraction as much."*

The Medical Device Tax Will Have Little Impact on the Medical Technology Industry

Christopher Flavelle

In the following viewpoint, a business analyst details the flaws in a study done by medical device maker AdvaMed that demonstrated negative economic effects from a forthcoming tax on medical devices. The author cites examples that show health-care spending remains stable even when prices rise. He argues that under the new tax, which is being enacted to underwrite the cost of broader public health coverage, demand for medical devices may actually rise because of the increase in health-care customers. Christopher Flavelle is an analyst for Bloomberg Government, a division of Bloomberg L.P.

As you read, consider the following questions:

1. According to Flavelle, how much money is the medical device tax expected to raise in the coming decade?

2. In the 2006 Mathematica Policy Research review, what percent did demand drop for every 10 percent increase in price?
3. To what false alarm from the 1980s does Flavelle compare AdvaMed's study?

The trade association for medical device makers such as Abbott Laboratories (ABT) and Medtronic (MDT) says a 2.3 percent excise tax on their products designed to help pay for the health-care overhaul will tank sales and push employment overseas. An industry-commissioned study concluded that "under reasonable assumptions," the tax would cost more than 43,000 U.S. jobs and shave as much as $6.7 billion off annual revenue of $116 billion.

A Bloomberg Government analysis finds the study is not credible. Its assumptions are flawed, in part because it exaggerates the degree to which spending on health is affected by price increases.

The tax, scheduled to go into effect in January 2013, covers items ranging from heart stents to artificial hips and is projected to raise $20 billion this decade to help pay the $1.5 trillion bill for expanding health coverage to the uninsured. The device industry's case against the levy was published last September [2011] by the Advanced Medical Technology Association, or AdvaMed, a Washington-based trade group. The findings have been cited by Republicans in Congress as a reason to repeal the levy. Representative Erik Paulsen of Minnesota, home to Medtronic, the world's largest maker of heart-rhythm devices, has introduced a bill to do that; it has 229 co-sponsors, including eight Democrats.

Yet AdvaMed's "reasonable assumptions" conflict with economic research, overstate companies' incentives to move jobs offshore, and ignore the positive effect of new demand created by the law.

The first assumption was that, if device makers passed part of the tax on to consumers, the resulting price increase could lead

The Medical Device Tax Will Have a Minimal Effect on Consumers

The effect of the excise tax on consumers' costs for health care and health insurance will be minimal and will be swamped by other factors. Spending on taxable medical devices represents less than 1 percent of total personal health expenditures, so a small increase in their price would have an almost imperceptible effect on health insurance premiums.

Paul N. Van de Water, "Excise Tax on
Medical Devices Should Not Be Repealed,"
Center on Budget and Policy Priorities,
May 31, 2012. www.cbpp.org.

to an equal or greater percentage decrease in sales—what economists would call elastic demand. Yet economic research shows that health-related spending is relatively inelastic: When prices go up, demand falls by only a fraction as much. A 2006 review of the economic literature by Mathematica Policy Research found an average elasticity of 0.2, meaning a 2 percent drop in demand for every 10 percent increase in price.

The industry study presented a much higher range of elasticity of demand, anywhere from 0.5 to 5. Bloomberg Government concludes that AdvaMed's estimates may overstate the revenue impact of the tax by up to a factor of 10. Using AdvaMed's lowest elasticity scenario, which is still higher than the economic literature suggests, the tax would trim revenue by $670 million, or about half of one percent of the industry's 2009 revenue.

The AdvaMed study also assumed the tax would create an incentive for device makers to shift their operations offshore, and posited, without citing evidence, that 10 percent of all U.S. jobs in the industry would flee. Yet under the new law, the tax will apply to all covered products—dialysis machines, pacemakers, heart monitors, and the like—sold in the U.S., regardless of where they are manufactured. Devices made in the U.S. for export are exempted from the tax. That means U.S. companies selling domestically have no new incentive to move production outside the country. Finally, the study assumed that none of the revenue lost by device makers would be offset by new demand, even though as many as 32 million Americans will be added to health insurers' rolls.

David Nexon, head of policy development at AdvaMed, said in an interview, "I don't want to defend the study methodology." But he said its prediction of job losses was "in the ballpark" and perhaps even low. He dismissed the economic research that shows demand for health care is relatively insensitive to rising costs, saying hospitals suffering cutbacks in federal reimbursements are likely to delay some purchases and resist price increases for others. And while he agreed that the newly insured will increase demand, he said most will be young adults, not the elderly who need more health care.

The device industry isn't the first to sound alarms over a policy it doesn't like. In the 1980s, the Motor Vehicle Manufacturers Association said requiring airbags in cars would raise costs, reduce sales, and sacrifice as many as 200,000 jobs. That did not happen.

Economic evidence supports the notion that the tax will reduce sales of medical devices. Yet the drop is likely to be less than AdvaMed predicts and could be offset by demand from millions of new customers—adding medical device makers to the list of interest groups that have fought government action, only to find their warnings were exaggerated.

Periodical and Internet Sources Bibliography

The following articles have been chosen to supplement the diverse views presented in this chapter.

Chris Arnold	"Sales Tax in Health Law Targets Medical Devices," *Morning Edition*, National Public Radio, July 2, 2012. www.npr.org.
Bill Crounse	"Don't Blame Technology for Driving Up the Cost of Health Care; Blame All of Us Who Use It Inappropriately," *MSDN HealthBlog*, March 7, 2012. http://blogs.msdn.com/b/healthblog.
John R. Graham	"Obamacare's Medical-Device Tax Kills Patients, Not Just Jobs," *Forbes*, June 6, 2012. www.forbes.com.
Adam Jutha	"Medicare and Medicaid Reforms That Can Help Curb Costs," National Academy of Social Insurance, May 24, 2012. www.nasi.org.
Yair Lotan and Joshua Sleeper	"Cost-Effectiveness of Robotic-Assisted Laparoscopic Procedures in Urologic Surgery in the USA," *Expert Review of Medical Devices*, vol. 8, no. 1, January 2011, p. 97.
John J. Smith, Tony R. Maida, Jennifer A. Agraz	"Medicare Coverage for New Medical Technology," *American Journal of Roentgenology*, vol. 176, no. 2, February 2001, pp. 313–316.
Christopher Weaver	"Excise Tax Remains for Medical Device Makers," *Wall Street Journal*, June 28, 2012. online.wsj.com.

CHAPTER 3

How Do Electronic Medical Records Impact Patients?

Chapter Preface

The US government has mandated all medical offices and hospitals to convert from paper records to electronic medical records (EMRs) by 2015. Although there is no industry standard, EMRs are generally self-contained databases of patient information maintained by individual hospitals and offices. These records will contain information about each patient visit, tests performed, results from treatments, and possibly digital images from X-rays and magnetic resonance imaging (MRIs). Some systems also provide treatment and drug interaction alerts based on the patient's condition. To maintain patient privacy, access to the records database is restricted to authorized personnel.

Although the Centers for Disease Control and Prevention reported in 2011 that 57 percent of office-based physicians have made the shift to EMRs, others are struggling with the cost, the technological infrastructure, and staff training in order to realize the full benefits of going digital. At first physicians were offered financial incentives by the government to convert to electronic systems, but after 2015, penalties in the form of annually snowballing decreases in Medicare reimbursements are intended to encourage EMR adoption.

Proponents of EMRs argue that the improved efficiency will inevitably lead to better care at a lower cost for patients, but these benefits are slow to materialize. In a 2012 video commentary, Bruce Cheson of *Medscape Hematology-Oncology* says doctors need to be mindful of the patient in the room with them and not be distracted by the computer and EMR. Cheson complains that the layout of the patient rooms forces him to choose to give his attention to either the patient or the computer. Dr. Pauline W. Chen shares a similar experience in a 2010 article for the *New York Times*. "Just because EMR improves information sharing and retrieval, it doesn't necessarily follow that our communication with patients and colleagues will also be better." Other doctors have reported seeing fewer patients or spending extra hours outside the normal workday getting caught up on entering data into the record system.

These obstacles are not insurmountable and are perhaps to be expected as part of a transition period, supporters note. EMRs have the potential to make it easier for patients to visit different doctors and have all of their medical history travel with them to each office. An industry standard or protocol is needed in order to make the transfer of patient information between offices and record systems go more smoothly, but this is viewed as an achievable goal. Having more access to one's medical record may also better engage patients with their care and treatment options, although security concerns loom large alongside this possibility. The ubiquity of EMRs is inevitable in the United States, but how this tool can be best used is still to be determined. In the following chapter, authors offer different perspectives on the benefits and drawbacks of EMRs.

> *"EMR [electronic medical records] is an extremely powerful tool when it comes to protecting patients from hospital errors."*

Electronic Medical Records Reduce Medical Error

Bernie Monegain

In the following viewpoint, a health-care journalist reports on the multi-million dollar savings at a Detroit-area hospital because of its electronic medical system. Huge improvements were noted in length of hospital stays, reduction in medical errors, and overall patient care, she writes. These improvements have set a precedent for other medical practices to follow suit in establishing an electronic medical system, she argues. Unfortunately, the author points out, hospitals that are not doing well financially are cutting back on information technology rather than investing in electronic medical records systems. Bernie Monegain is an editor at MedTech Media.

As you read, consider the following questions:

1. According to the author, in what year did the Detroit Medical Center begin implementing its electronic medical system?

2. According to Monegain, what percentage of medication errors has been reduced through use of electronic medical systems at the Detroit Medical Center?
3. What is the Detroit Medical Center saving due to the shorter stays of patients suffering from pressure ulcers, according to Monegain?

Detroit Medical Center executives say they have achieved improved patient safety and saved $5 million to boot, thanks to DMC's system-wide electronic medical system.

It is the second year in a row in which computer-based healthcare information processing created major improvements in quality of care and cost-savings for DMC's eight hospitals, officials said.

The windfall in savings—triggered by highly effective electronic monitoring of critical tasks such as treating pressure ulcers and preventing medication errors—resulted in a healthy return on investment, they said.

The $50 million system powered by Kansas City, Mo.–based Cerner Corp, has gone online throughout the DMC in gradual stages over a 12-year period, starting in 1998.

"The latest numbers are in, and we continue to see great strides in improving quality, treating patients more quickly and preventing error, which translates to dollar savings as well," said Chief Nursing Officer Patricia Natale. "This work with these results is very exciting."

"The savings are only part of the story," she added, "because EMR [electronic medical records] is also a major step forward on the road to better quality of patient care. Thanks to EMR, we're now seeing a dramatic reduction in the length of hospital stays due to pressure sores, along with a dramatic reduction of drug errors through EMR-enabled medication scanning."

"The latest surveys show that EMR has helped to reduce medication errors by up to 75 percent," said DMC Chief Medical

Information Officer Leland Babitch, MD. "Obviously, that's a major gain for patients—especially given the fact that medication errors account for the majority of accidental deaths and injuries at U.S. hospitals."

The U.S. Institute of Medicine has estimated that up to 100,000 patients die as a result of hospital errors annually.

Treating Pressure Ulcers

The impact of the electronic medical record system on the treatment of pressure ulcers was especially noticeable, said DMC quality-of-care administrators.

They noted that the chronic sores often require extended hospital stays and thus drive up costs. But the most recent DMC Patient Care Services study of severe pressure ulcer cases showed that close EMR monitoring of bedsores reduced the average length of stay required to treat them by nearly three full days last year, compared with the average length of ulcer-triggered stays before EMR monitoring began in 2008.

The DMC study concluded that the reduction in the length of pressure ulcer-related hospital stays—in a system that admits more than 75,000 patients each year—was now helping to generate more than $4.5 million in yearly cost savings.

"The data on electronic medical records and patient safety and quality of care are clear and convincing by now," said DMC Vice President for Quality and Safety Michelle Schreiber, MD. "Those data demonstrate beyond a reasonable doubt that EMR is an extremely powerful tool when it comes to protecting patients from hospital errors.

"But EMR is also proving to be an effective method for promoting quality of care—and the new numbers on bedsores and length of stays show how computer-based recordkeeping helps caregivers to take better care of patients day in and day out."

In spite of the savings to be had from hospital-based EMR, however, recent studies show that the majority of U.S. hospitals have either failed to implement top-to-bottom EMR systems—

Electronic Medical Records Improve Patient Care

In the 18 months after the [electronic medical record] system went live hospital-wide in June 2006 [at Midland Memorial in Texas], the hospital reduced medication errors and patient deaths. Infection rates dropped 88% thanks to guidelines in the record system that prompted nurses to follow infection-control procedures, such as changing a dressing or following correct procedures when inserting a new IV.

Laura Landro, "An Affordable Fix for Modernizing Medical Records," Wall Street Journal, *April 30, 2009. online.wsj.com.*

or are cutting back on information technology (IT) programs already in place.

As of August 2010, fewer than 4 percent of U.S. hospitals had implemented the level of system-wide electronic patient record-keeping that is now in place at the DMC. In addition, a recent study at the University of Michigan School of Medicine showed that more than one-fourth of the nation's recession-affected hospitals have been cutting back on their already existing IT programs.

The cash-strapped hospitals were slashing IT budgets, reported the study in the *Journal of Hospital Medicine,* in spite of the fact that the Obama administration has recently made available more than $2.73 billion in Medicare/Medicaid bonuses for clinicians and hospitals that spend to improve their electronic medical records systems.

"The DMC has spent $50 million on building a powerful EMR system over the past five or six years," said Michael Duggan, president and CEO of the Detroit Medical Center, "and we did it because we like to think of ourselves as the 'hospital of the future'—as a state-of-the-art healing center where patients know they can get the best healthcare available anywhere today."

"At the same time, the ability to greatly reduce healthcare costs via electronic medical records is an added bonus—which makes implementing EMR a win-win situation for everyone involved."

| "More than one in five hospital medication errors . . . were caused at least partly by computers."

Electronic Medical Records Increase Medical Error

Alexi Mostrous

In the following viewpoint, a journalist reports on studies that undermine the widely held belief that electronic medical records improve patient safety. According to the author, electronic records have led to dosage errors, diagnostic errors, and even confusion of units of measure. Despite concerns, many health professionals still believe that overall patient care has improved, the author writes. He maintains that hospitals and health information technology organizations need incentive to report problems they are experiencing with their electronic medical records systems to improve accountability. Alexi Mostrous is a staff writer for the Washington Post.

As you read, consider the following questions:

1. According to Mostrous, what percentage of hospitals has at least a basic electronic medical system?

2. How many hours did emergency room physicians at St. Mary Mercy Hospital spend on a computer, according to the viewpoint?

3. How many paper-based errors were reported to Quantros Inc. in 2008, as compared to computer-based errors, as cited in the viewpoint?

When President [Barack] Obama designated $19.5 billion to expand the use of electronic medical records, former House speaker Newt Gingrich (R-Ga.) said it was one of only "two good things" in February's stimulus package.

But such bipartisan enthusiasm has obscured questions about the effectiveness of health information technology [IT] products, critics say. Interviews with more than two dozen doctors, academics, patients and computer programmers suggest that computer systems can increase errors, add hours to doctors' workloads and compromise patient care.

"Health IT can be beneficial, but many current systems are clunky, counterintuitive and in some cases dangerous," said Ross Koppel, a sociologist at the University of Pennsylvania School of Medicine who published a key study on electronic medical records in 2005.

Under the stimulus program, hospitals and physicians can claim millions of dollars for IT purchases, and will be penalized if they do not go digital by 2015. Obama has said the changes will save billions and will minimize medication errors.

But health IT's effectiveness is unclear. Researchers at the University of Minnesota found in March [2009] that electronic records prevented only two infections a year. A 2005 report in the journal *Pediatrics* found that deaths at the children's hospital at the University of Pittsburgh Medical Center more than doubled in the five months after a computerized order-entry system went online. UPMC said the study had not found that technology caused the rise in mortality and maintained that medication errors were down 60 percent since computers were introduced in 2002.

Others studies have concluded that health IT saves time and reduces errors. It has been used successfully in organizations such as the Department of Veterans Affairs and Kaiser Permanente.

Documenting the Flaws in Electronic Medical Records Systems

However, the Senate Finance Committee has amassed a thick file of testimony alleging serious computer flaws from doctors, patients and engineers unhappy with current systems.

On Oct. 16, the panel wrote to 10 major sellers of electronic record systems, demanding to know, for example, what steps they had taken to safeguard patients. "Every accountability measure ought to be used to track the stimulus money invested in health information technology," said Sen. Charles E. Grassley (Iowa), the panel's ranking Republican.

Anonymous reports sent to the Joint Commission, the body charged with certifying 17,000 health-care organizations; Grassley's staff; and the Food and Drug Administration disclose problems, including:

- Faulty software that miscalculated intracranial pressures and mixed up kilograms and pounds.
- A computer system that systematically gave adult doses of medications to children.
- An IT program designed to warn physicians about wrong dosages that was disconnected when the vendor updated the system, leading to incorrect dosing.
- A software bug that misdiagnosed five people with herpes.

David Blumenthal, the head of health technology at the Department of Health and Human Services, acknowledged that the systems had flaws. "But the critical question is whether, on balance, care is better than before," he said. "I think the answer is yes."

Ignoring Clinical Alerts Leads to Medical Error

[Electronic health records' (EHRs)] clinical alerts . . . [are] supposed to improve care by automatically warning physicians about potential drug interactions, overdosing, allergies, or other hazards resulting from the orders they enter. "Eighty to 90 percent of alerts are overridden," says [Ross] Koppel, [a University of Pennsylvania sociologist] who's also on the faculty of Penn's medical school. Experienced physicians often find alerts annoying and intrusive. Koppel works with residents, who commonly rotate among several hospitals and EHRs. Each system's alerts may be based on different criteria, or turned off entirely.

"A resident will get an alert at 50 [milligrams of a certain drug] at one hospital, 60 at a second hospital, and no alert at a third hospital because they turned it off."

Elizabeth Gardner, "Danger: EHRs Can Replace One Set of Medical Errors for Another," Health Data Management, *vol. 18, no. 8, August 1, 2010, p. 30.*

Over the next two months, Blumenthal will finalize the definition of "meaningful use," the standard that hospitals and physicians will have to reach before qualifying for health IT stimulus funds. He would not say whether applicants would have to submit adverse-event reports, a safety net that many doctors and academics have called for but that vendors have resisted.

"If you look at other high-risk industries, like drug regulation or aviation, there's a requirement to report problems," said David C. Classen, an associate professor of medicine at the University of Utah who recently completed a study on health IT installations.

Rates of Use Remain Low and Complaints Are Frequent

Today, barely 8 percent of hospitals have even a basic electronic medical system. Only 17 percent of physicians use electronic records, and many of those are uninstalling them, including 20 percent of physician groups in Arizona, according to a June survey by HealthLeaders-InterStudy.

Outside the United States, countries further along the digital curve have experienced major problems with American-made health IT systems.

In Britain, a $20 billion program to digitalize medicine across the National Health Service is five years behind schedule and heavily over budget. A British parliamentary committee in January criticized the vendor, Cerner, as "not providing value for money."

Sarah Bond, a Cerner spokeswoman, said patient safety had improved and errors had dropped at U.S. hospitals that used Cerner products.

Cerner's stock price has risen 122 percent since February. Shares in Allscripts, another major health IT player whose chief executive, Glen E. Tullman, served on Obama's campaign finance committee, rose by 126 percent over the same period.

But rising share prices have not always translated into better care.

"It's been a complete nightmare," said Steve Chabala, an emergency room physician at St. Mary Mercy Hospital in Livonia, Mich., which switched to electronic records three years ago. "I can't see my patients because I'm at a screen entering data."

Last year, his department found that physicians spent nearly five of every 10 hours on a computer, he said. "I sit down and log on to a computer 60 times every shift. Physician productivity and satisfaction have fallen off a cliff."

Other doctors spoke of cluttered screens, unresponsive vendors and illogical displays. "It's a huge safety issue," said Christine Sinsky, an internist in Dubuque, Iowa, whose practice implemented electronic records six years ago. "I can't tell from the medical display whether a patient is receiving 4mg or 8mg of a certain drug. It took us two years to get a back-button on our [electronic health record] (EHR) browser."

She emphasized that electronic records have improved her practice. "We wouldn't want to go back," she said. "But EHRs are still in need of significant improvement."

More than one in five hospital medication errors reported last year—27,969 out of 133,662—were caused at least partly by computers, according to data submitted by 379 hospitals to Quantros Inc., a health-care information company. Paper-based errors caused 10,954 errors, the data showed.

Tracking Health Mishaps Caused by Electronic Medical Records

Legal experts say it is impossible to know how often health IT mishaps occur. Electronic medical records are not classified as medical devices, so hospitals are not required to report problems. Many health IT contracts do not allow hospitals to discuss computer flaws, say Koppel and Sharona Hoffman, a professor of law and bioethics at Case Western Reserve University in Cleveland.

"Doctors who report problems can lose their jobs," Hoffman said. "Hospitals don't have any incentive to do so and may be in breach of contract if they do."

For one senior internist at a major hospital, who requested anonymity because he said he would lose his job if he went public, a 2006 installation provoked mayhem. "The system crashed soon after it went online," he said. "I walked in to find no records on any patients. It was like being on the moon without oxygen."

While orange-shirted vendor employees "ran around with no idea how to work their own equipment," the internist said, doctors struggled to keep chronically ill patients alive. "I didn't go through all my training to have my ability to take care of patients destroyed by devices that are an impediment to medical care."

"Around the country, medical identity theft is one of the fastest growing forms of identity fraud, with more than 5 million people affected in 2010 alone."

Growing Medical Identity Theft Puts Patients at Risk

Liv Osby

In the following viewpoint, a journalist reports on the growing concern for the security of electronic medical records. The push to implement electronic medical records has rushed ahead of security measures, she argues, making electronic records more vulnerable than their paper counterparts. To make matters worse, she claims, electronic records are usually breached by an internal user, thus necessary security measures are complex. Nonetheless, she asserts, there are no industry standards regarding limited access to records, data encryption, and password protection. Until security standards are in place, medical identity theft will continue to thrive in an electronic world, she concludes. Liv Osby is a staff writer specializing in medical issues for the Greenville News *in South Carolina.*

As you read, consider the following questions:

1. What are the consequences for people whose electronic medical records are breached, as described by Osby?
2. According to Osby, how many more times are electronic medical records breached than paper records?
3. How many people have been affected by breaches of electronic medical records since 2009, according to Osby?

Allegations of a theft scam involving patient records at Greenville Hospital System surfaced recently, while personal data at Spartanburg Regional Healthcare System was potentially compromised last year when a laptop computer was stolen.

Around the country, medical identity theft is one of the fastest growing forms of identity fraud, with more than 5 million people affected in 2010 alone, according to the U.S. Department of Health and Human Services.

Mark Savage, a senior attorney for Consumers Union, told GreenvilleOnline.com the breach of people's personal electronic health information is a cause for concern.

"The problem for consumers is getting the benefits while protecting the privacy and security of that information," Savage said.

Electronic medical records have the potential to improve people's health as well as the efficiency of the health care system.

But with the name, address, date of birth, Social Security number and other personal information, it's also a wealth of data for potential identity thieves, who can use it to defraud hospitals or for other financial gain.

That can leave patients with bills for medical services they never received, jeopardize their credit, leave them open to the wrong treatment because of incorrect medical information, or even face the loss of a job should sensitive medical information be revealed.

PricewaterhouseCoopers's Health Research Institute recently surveyed 600 health care providers, insurers and other industry groups and found that medical identity theft is on the rise.

But security efforts haven't kept pace with the growth in electronic records, data sharing, and social media and mobile technology to manage patient data, or the new uses for digital health information.

More than a third of hospitals and physician groups reported patients using another identity to get services, but fewer than half of those groups had polices governing the use of mobile devices and social media, according to the survey.

Meanwhile, a quarter of insurers improperly transferred files with sensitive data, PricewaterhouseCoopers reported.

Jennifer Gregg, a regulatory affairs assistant from Greenville, said her personal information, along with her 5-year-old daughter's, was on a laptop that was stolen, leaving her feeling "violated" and afraid for her daughter's future credit record.

"You hear so often that these medical companies are losing this information," said Gregg, 35. "They should use other means (than Social Security numbers) to identify you. And there needs to be limited access to this information."

Data breaches have been reported at facilities from VA hospitals to private clinics.

Theft is the most common cause of breaches involving 500 or more patients, followed by intentional unauthorized access to or use of health information, human error, and loss of electronic media or paper records, HHS reports.

Though paper records can be accessed, electronic breaches occur three times as often and affect 25 times more people, according to PricewaterhouseCoopers.

More than half the health organizations in the PricewaterhouseCoopers survey, conducted over two years, reported at least one data privacy or security issue, with improper use by an internal party as the top problem.

At GHS, where an employee was charged by the Greenville County Sheriff's Office with financial identity fraud after authorities alleged that she used her access to records for financial gain, patient confidentiality is a top priority, said Skip Morris, executive director of corporate integrity.

The employee, a patient care technician, was suspended without pay.

The hospital has "one of the strictest disciplinary policies in the country" for employees who breach patient privacy, Morris said.

"GHS constantly evaluates information security controls and strengthens those controls as technology changes," he said. "In recent years, we have encrypted email, encrypted all laptops and also recently encrypted mobile devices that access GHS systems."

Morris said the investigation is continuing and that GHS will contact patients whose information may have been breached and provide credit monitoring and restoration service to those adversely affected.

At Spartanburg Regional, where an information security council was formed last year to ensure that policies protecting patient information are consistent and strong, there have been "vigorous improvements" in the safety of electronic and paper records, spokesman Chad Lawson said.

"As technology grows and changes and becomes even more vital to the continuing development of improved quality, we must promise that our efforts to keep information safe are adaptable to the fast growth of electronic medical records and other portals for speed and efficiency in patient care," he said.

"Our internal dialogue about the safety and security of sensitive personal information has never been more robust, and we have faith in our strengthened approach."

Lawson said the hospital has no evidence that anyone was harmed by last year's breach but added that affected patients were given access to free credit monitoring services.

According to PricewaterhouseCoopers, digitized health data today are also being shared by a variety of organizations and business partners, though few have established proper restrictions to control access.

And that's the source of more than half of reported breaches, affecting more than 11 million people since 2009, Pricewater-houseCoopers reported.

So health organizations must update practices and adopt more integrated approaches to keep information out of the wrong hands, it concluded.

Sen. Al Franken, D-Minn., who chairs the Senate Subcommittee on Privacy, Technology and the Law, said at a hearing in November that more than 18 million Americans have been affected by health privacy breaches since 2009 and that more needs to be done to protect the data.

Savage said Consumers Union has developed a set of principles that cover privacy and security, misuse of data and accountability.

First, he said, the industry must limit those who have access, encrypt all data, and employ password protection and user codes. It also should have audit trails, which are accessible to patients, to track use and flag inappropriate activity, he said.

"We have been pushing that patients should have the right to review their own information," he said.

Furthermore, he said, doctors should request the minimum information needed to treat a patient and hold it only as long as necessary.

And they should use it only for the purpose they collect it for, not for marketing or any other reason, he said.

Additionally, he said, patients must be given the opportunity for meaningful consent for use of their data instead of simply checking a box when they need treatment.

Gregg, a mother of two who now checks her credit report annually, said she'd like to see better solutions for people whose information has been breached along with any extra steps to protect personal information.

"If someone has it," she said, "they can do a lot of damage."

> "The majority of Americans are aware
> of the benefits of electronic records
> and believe that they outweigh privacy
> concerns."

Electronic Medical Records Do Not Increase Identity Theft

Linda Thede

In the following viewpoint, an informatics specialist ponders the question of whether electronic health records (EHRs) are a great benefit or a privacy nightmare when compared to paper medical records. EHRs are additionally protected by authentication and the audit trail of who has accessed the record, she argues. Health Insurance Portability and Accountability Act (HIPAA) regulations give patients the right to receive information about who has accessed their EHRs and when, she maintains. The author concludes that for most Americans the benefits of EHRs outweigh the risks. Linda Thede is the editor of CIN Plus, *an insert to* CIN: Computers, Informatics, Nursing.

As you read, consider the following questions:

1. According to Thede, which are more secure, electronic or paper medical records?

2. What legislation extended the HIPAA Privacy Rules?
3. According to Thede, what is the difference between an electronic medical record and an electronic health record?

To answer this question, let's start by saying that, depending on how the data is used, it can be either. So the question is, to what extent can we garner the benefits of an electronic health record (EHR) while maintaining data privacy? Most of us are aware that the risk to privacy of any information increases exponentially with each additional person whom we tell. This is especially true for electronic communication. Social networking members, who have shared what they thought was private information with "friends," have too often found that the information is now accessible far beyond what they ever imagined; now it is permanently engraved in cyberworld. These observations rightly raise concerns when information in a medical record is involved.

People are asking whether any kind of electronic records can be made safe. If one is looking for a 100% privacy guarantee, the answer is no. But then, paper records are not 100% secure either. There have been cases where paper medical records, especially parts of them, have disappeared. There was a case where boxes of patient records from a doctor's office were found in a garbage dumpster (Preventing Medical Identity Theft, 2008) and a case in which stolen medical records were recently found washed up on a Maine shore (Associated Press, 2008b). Additionally, disposing of paper records can be a privacy breach as a teacher in Salt Lake City, who had purchased medical records from 28 Florida hospitals to use as scrap paper for her students, learned (Associated Press, 2008a).

On a hospital unit, a patient's paper record (chart) is often available to anyone with a white coat, a badge that looks like the identification badge of the agency, and the courage to pick up the chart. With an electronic record, it is more difficult for an unauthorized person to gain access to a healthcare record. To do so a person needs more than a white coat and a badge; the person also needs a login name and a password. Additionally, electronic record systems maintain an audit trail, required by the privacy rules of the Health Insurance Portability and Accountability Act (HIPAA), that records who has accessed what record, as well as what part of the record was viewed. In contrast, in a paper record, neither the person who has accessed a record, nor what the person accessed is known.

Given the relative ease of access of electronic records for those with the appropriate login, and the fact that login audit trails only work when they are routinely examined, it is possible for an unauthorized person to access a record, resulting in a concern about the privacy of information in healthcare records. This possibility takes on a new note of concern in a facility in which one is both a patient and an employee. This fear was expressed by a reader who responded to an earlier *OJIN* Informatics Column about the electronic health record (Thede, 2008, August 18). Because it is possible for decisions about firing and hiring to be made based on healthcare information found in an employee's, or a potential employee's record, access to a person's healthcare record is a legitimate concern for everyone. The question then becomes "Will administrative personnel have access to an individual employee's records?" The answer is legally "no." Yet in reality, unless the audit trails are examined by individuals independent of any administrative oversight, this access could remain secret. Keep in mind, however, that a paper record is also fair game for a "snooping-minded" individual, and in this case there is no record of any access.

Fortunately, today there are more protections against this type of snooping, as well as other risks to privacy breaches, than in the past. HIPAA, although its primary purpose was to insure the portability of healthcare information, recognized that data in an electronic format can be easily shared. To protect this data, rules were promulgated to set a national standard for the privacy of health information. These rules took effect April 14, 2003.

Although these rules were an excellent start, they fell ". . . far short of providing adequate protection either in the traditional healthcare arena or for the rapidly evolving e-health environment" (Center for Democracy and Technology, 2009).

Under the original HIPAA Privacy Rules individuals had the right to request an "accounting of disclosures" of one's identifiable health information for a period of six years prior to the date of the request. The right, however, was limited because it excluded disclosures for treatment, payment, and business operations. The American Recovery and Reinvestment Act of 2009 (ARRA), signed into law by President Obama in February 2009, contained the Health Information Technology for Economic and Clinical Health Act (HITECH) which extends these rules (HIPPA.com, 2009). The rules now require that a covered entity that maintains electronic health records has to account for disclosures for purposes of treatment, payment, and business operations for three years prior to the date of the request (Section 13405). However, unless a person requests this information, the individual will not be told that the record has been accessed. Thus, if nurses think that their healthcare record has been improperly accessed to prevent them from being hired or promoted, they can find out if this is true. The same is not true for a paper record.

One of the main problems under the original HIPAA rules was that they were not clear on the responsibilities of "business associates." A business associate is an individual or group that contracts with healthcare providers to perform specific services, such as billing or developing electronic healthcare records. Business entities were obligated to comply with privacy rules only to the extent required in their contracts (Center for Democracy and Technology, 2009). Thus, if a contract with a healthcare agency for an electronic medical record did not specify that the agency owned the data, it was possible for the vendor to misuse this data. ARRA specifies that now ". . . business associates must abide by nearly all of the HIPAA regulations on data

Paper Records Are Not More Secure than Electronic Medical Records

With the threat of identity theft and hackers, many people fear putting their personal information into an electronic system, says Andy Salmen, who works in business development at Healthcare Information Services, a Chicago-based company.

"If someone wanted to steal your medical records, it would be easier to throw a brick through your doctor's office window than to steal them electronically," he says.

Carroll Cole, "Bringing Healthcare Up to Speed," Chicago Health, *chicagohealthonline.com.*

security (Section 13401); must directly comply with all of the new privacy provisions enacted in ARRA (Section 13404); and can be held directly accountable for failure to comply with any HIPAA Privacy Rule provisions in their work with covered entities (Section 13404)" (Center for Democracy and Technology, 2009). For more information about these regulations see Majority Staff of the Committees (2009). Privacy rules apply to healthcare records whether they are electronic medical records (EMR), or electronic health records (EHR). An EMR is an electronic healthcare record under the ownership of a single entity, such as a private healthcare practitioner or a healthcare institution. An EHR is an individual's healthcare record from different healthcare agencies from which, when requested by the patient, selected portions can be shared with other agencies (National Alliance for Health Information Technology, 2008). The new rules also apply to regional healthcare data-sharing organizations, such as the Regional Health Information Organization (RHIO) in Boston that shares information in medical records for the purpose of improving healthcare.

Although Americans are concerned about the privacy of medical records, survey data shows that despite this concern, the majority of Americans are aware of the benefits of electronic records and believe that they outweigh privacy concerns (Bright, 2007). They are eager to benefit from them for a number of reasons including the belief that use of electronic medical records can improve the quality of care by reducing the number of redundant or unnecessary tests and procedures they receive as well as reduce medical errors and healthcare costs. Additionally, the survey showed that people believe that the ability to share information can result in better care. As patients age it also becomes more difficult for them to remember all the information that might be pertinent for a given provider. Actually anyone who has struggled to locate, for referral purposes, medical records located in a variety of different provider offices finds the thought of a full EHR very appealing.

To answer the question posed by the title, despite opposition from those who have a vested interest in not having an EHR, or even an EMR, such as drug companies whose drugs are creating previously uncovered side effects, or agencies that make money by repeating lab tests, electronic health records are a plus. This does not mean that efforts to protect healthcare data should be lessened. It does mean that we need to acknowledge the considerable progress already made in protecting healthcare data and the progress that will continue to be made. No, the records will never be 100% safe; but the benefits outweigh the risks, and no information, once shared, is ever 100% safe from disclosure.

References

Associated Press. (2008a, March 10). Medical Records Sold to Teacher as Scrap Paper. Retrieved February 8, 2010, from www.msnbc.msn.com/id/23561667/

Associated Press. (2008b, Nov 17). Stolen Maine hospital records found. Retrieved February 8, 2010, from www.seacoastonline.com/articles/20081117-NEWS-81117005

Bright, B. (2007, November 29). Benefits of Electronic Health Records Seen as Outweighing Privacy Risks Retrieved February 10, 2010, from http://online.wsj.com/article/SB119565244262500549.html

Center for Democracy and Technology. (2009, March 27). Improvements and Challenges in Health Privacy Law. Retrieved January 21, 2010, from www.cdt.org/policy/improvements-and-challenges-health-privacy-law

HIPPA.com. (2009). ARRA's HITECH Privacy Provisions Apply HIPAA Security Rule to Business Associates. Retrieved January 21, 2010, from www.hipaa.com/2009/02/arras-hitech-privacy-provisions-apply-hipaa-security-rule-to-business-associates/

Majority Staff of the Committees on Energy and Commerce Ways and Means, a. S. a. T. (2009, January 16). Health Information Technology for Economic and Clinical Health Act or HITECH Act.Retrieved November 13, 2009, from http://waysandmeans.house.gov/media/pdf/110/hit2.pdf.

National Alliance for Health Information Technology. (2008, April 28). Defining Key Health Information Technology Terms. Retrieved January 21, 2010, from http://healthit.hhs.gov/portal/server.pt/gateway/PTARGS_0_10741_848133_0_0_18/10_2_hit_terms.pdf

Preventing Medical Identity Theft. (2008). Retrieved February 9, 2010, from http://press room.shredit.com/uploads/White%20Papers/Medical%20Case%20Study%20July%202009.pdf

Thede, L. (2008, August 18, 2008). The Electronic Health Record: Will Nursing Be on Board When the Ship Leaves? *OJIN: The Online Journal of Issues in Nursing* Retrieved 3, 13, from www.nursingworld.org/MainMenuCategories/ANAMarketplace/ANAPeriodicals/OJIN/Columns/Informatics/ElectronicHealthRecord.aspx

Periodical and Internet Sources Bibliography

The following articles have been chosen to supplement the diverse views presented in this chapter.

David Bailey	"Identity Theft Check Up: Electronic Medical Records Are the New Credit Cards," *Redspin*, March 3, 2010. www.redspin.com.
Cristen Conger	"Are Electronic Medical Records Safe?," *Discovery News*, May 26, 2010. http://news.discovery.com.
Shelley DuBois	"Electronic Medical Records: Great, But Not Very Private," *CNN Money*, October 6, 2010. http://money.cnn.com.
Margalit Gur-Arie	"How EMR and EHR Systems Can Kill Patients," *KevinMD.com*, June 2010. www.kevinmd.com/blog.
Angela Haupt	"The Era of Electronic Medical Records," *U.S. News & World Report*, July 18, 2011. http://health.usnews.com.
Steve Lohr	"Digital Records May Not Cut Health Costs, Study Cautions," *New York Times*, March 5, 2012. www.nytimes.com.
Rick McMullen	"Badly Design Electronic Medical Records Can Kill You," *Fast Co. Design*, August 17, 2011. www.fastcodesign.com.
Mary Shedden	"Conversion to Electronic Medical Records Going Slowly," *Tampa Bay Online*, March 25, 2012. www2.tbo.com.
Larry Walsh	"Study: EMR Driving Up Health Care Costs," *Channelnomics*, March 7, 2012. http://channelnomics.com.

CHAPTER 4

What Is the Government's Role in Medical Technology?

Chapter Preface

The US Food and Drug Administration (FDA) was formed in the early twentieth century with the purpose of ensuring the safety of products that Americans use. Prior to the establishment of the FDA, which was first known as the Bureau of Chemistry in the Department of Agriculture, there was little regulation of products such as food and medicine, which often lead to death and injury.

The FDA's regulatory powers grew significantly after the thalidomide tragedy of the 1950s. In Europe, thalidomide was prescribed as a sleeping pill and then later found to cause terrible birth defects. Thalidomide was not available in the United States because FDA medical officer Dr. Frances Kelsey had concerns about its safety. Kelsey's cautiousness bolstered public support of the FDA and its regulatory power; a few years later, in 1962, the Kefauver-Harris Drug Amendments to the Federal Food, Drug, and Cosmetic Act were passed, requiring drug manufacturers to demonstrate a new drug's efficacy and safety to the FDA before it could be marketed.

In 1976, the FDA began supervising the regulation of medical devices after passage of the Medical Device Amendment to the Federal Food, Drug, and Cosmetic Act. These amendments established the three classes of medical devices, based on patient risk, used by the FDA in regulation. The amendments also required manufacturers to register their medical devices with the FDA. The Safe Medical Devices Act of 1990 required hospitals and other medical facilities to report any injury or death attributable to a medical device to the FDA and the device manufacturer. Although laws about reporting already existed, government studies showed that reportage was as low as one percent, spurring the passage of the 1990 legislation.

Since the formalizing of the FDA's regulatory process, there has always been a push-and-pull between the government and medical device manufacturers. The government wants safety, while the manufacturers want their products on the market quickly. The FDA has been accused of taking too long to approve treatments and therefore costing people their lives. In a 2011 article for the *Wall Street Journal*, "How the FDA Could Cost You Your Life," Scott Gottlieb outlines the disparity between US and European regulation of medical devices. Gottlieb argues that Europe's modern regulatory process is just as safe, yet twice as fast. The FDA has responded to critics with some flexibility. Its 501(k) process was put in place to fast-track moderate-risk devices that are substantially equivalent to devices already on the market, but this process has also been criticized as unsafe.

The tug-of-war between safe and fast regulation continues to impact the medical field. In the following chapter, authors debate the government's role in medical technology.

"*The US system has served patients well by preventing EU-approved devices that were later shown to be unsafe or ineffective from harming American consumers.*"

Regulation of Medical Technology Protects Patients and Is Becoming More Efficient

Jeffrey Shuren

In the following viewpoint, a US Food and Drug Administration (FDA) representative delivers a statement before the Subcommittee on Health. He contends that the FDA is a world leader in vetting new medical devices. While some concern has been expressed that devices take too long to come to market in the United States, he maintains that the FDA's high standards have protected Americans from poor quality products. Jeffrey Shuren is the director of the Center for Devices and Radiological Health at the FDA.

Jeffrey Shuren, "Impact of Medical Device Regulation on Jobs and Patients," Statement Before the Subcommittee on Health, Committee on Energy and Commerce, US House of Representatives, February 17, 2011.

As you read, consider the following questions:

1. According to Shuren, what significant task is the FDA charged with?
2. What percentage of reviews did the FDA complete in ninety days in 2010, according to Shuren?
3. How many women were affected, according to Shuren, by a 2010 breast implant recall in Europe?

Mr. Chairman and Members of the Subcommittee, I am Dr. Jeffrey Shuren, Director of the Center for Devices and Radiological Health (CDRH) at the Food and Drug Administration (FDA or the Agency). Thank you for the opportunity to discuss the effects of medical device regulation on jobs and patients. FDA recognizes the many important contributions that the medical device industry makes to the economy and to the public health. By increasing the predictability, consistency, and transparency of our regulatory pathways, we can help provide better treatments and diagnostics to patients more quickly, stimulate investment in and development of promising new technologies to meet critical public health needs, and increase the global market position of US medical devices.

The Background on Regulatory Authorities for Medical Devices

I will begin with a brief overview of our regulatory authorities for medical devices. A medical device, as defined by federal law, encompasses several thousand health products, from simple articles such as tongue depressors and heating pads, to cutting-edge and complex devices such as implantable defibrillators and robotic equipment for minimally invasive surgery.

The Medical Device Amendments of 1976 to the Federal Food, Drug, and Cosmetic Act (FD&C Act or the Act) gave FDA specific authority to regulate the safety and effectiveness of medical devices. Medical devices are assigned to one of three regulatory classes based on risk.

Class I, General Controls, is the lowest risk category of devices and includes items such as adhesive bandages. These devices are subject to the General Controls of the Act, which include establishment registration and device listing, compliance with current Good Manufacturing Practice (cGMP) and labeling, record-keeping, and reporting requirements.

Class II, Special Controls, is a medium-risk category of devices and includes devices such as intravenous catheters and powered wheelchairs. They are subject to the General Controls of the Act as well as Special Controls, which may include special labeling requirements, mandatory performance standards, and post-market surveillance, in order to ensure device safety and effectiveness.

Class III is the highest risk category of devices and includes devices such as heart valves and coronary stents. These devices are subject to the General Controls of the Act, plus approval prior to marketing of a premarket approval application (PMA) containing scientific evidence of the device's safety and effectiveness.

Most devices, however, are cleared via the premarket notification [510(k)] process. A 510(k) is a premarket submission to demonstrate that the device to be marketed is "substantially equivalent" to another legally marketed (predicate) device. If a device otherwise subject to premarket review is not substantially equivalent to another legally marketed device, it must go through either the PMA process or the "de novo" classification process (a review process for innovative, lower-risk products).

The Impact of Regulation on Innovation

FDA is charged with a significant task: to protect and promote the health of the American public. To succeed in that mission, we must ensure the safety and effectiveness of the medical products that Americans rely on every day, and also facilitate the scientific innovations that make these products safer, more effective, and more affordable.

These dual roles have a profound effect on the nation's economy. FDA medical device approval gives manufacturers a worldwide base of consumer confidence. Our ability to work with innovators to translate discoveries into approvable products in a timely way is essential to the growth of the medical products industry and the jobs it creates. US-based companies dominate the roughly $350 billion global medical device industry. The US medical device industry is one of the few sectors in these challenging economic times with a positive trade balance. In 2000, the US medical device industry ranked thirteenth in venture capital investment—now, ten years later, it's our country's fourth largest sector for venture capital investment.

As noted in a January 2011 report on medical technology innovation by PwC (formerly PricewaterhouseCoopers), the US regulatory system and US regulatory standard have served American industry and patients well. As that report states, "U.S. success in medical technology during recent decades stems partially from global leadership of the US Food and Drug Administration. FDA's standards and guidelines to ensure safety and efficacy have instilled confidence in the industry's products worldwide. Other countries' regulators often wait to see FDA's position before acting on medical technology applications, and often model their own regulatory approach on FDA's."

FDA's Device Review Performance Is Strong

Some have alleged that delays in FDA approval deprive American patients of needed therapies and push jobs overseas. Yet, as FDA's FY [fiscal year] 2010 Medical Device User Fee Act Performance Report to Congress indicates, FDA's device review performance has been consistently strong. Ninety-five percent of the over 4,000 medical device applications subject to user fees that FDA reviews every year (FDA reviews over 9,000 submissions annually in total) are reviewed within the goals that were agreed to by the medical device industry under the Medical Device User Fee Amendments of 2007 (MDUFA). Under the 510(k) program—the pathway used by 90 percent of the devices we examine each year—90 percent of our reviews were completed in 90 days or less, and 98 percent of reviews were completed in 150 days or less, as we committed to do under MDUFA.

There are a limited number of areas in which we are not meeting the goals agreed to with the industry, although our performance in those areas is generally improving. This is the result of several factors, including increasing workload, turnover of key staff, growing device complexity, and poor-quality submissions. The number of applications for premarket approval and panel-track supplements (for "breakthrough" devices) has increased by 48 percent over the past two years. In addition, medical devices are becoming more technologically complex, as reflected by the growing number and variety of technical experts that FDA must consult during the review process. Finally, a significant number of submissions received by the Agency are incomplete or fail to address basic elements such as the device's proposed indications for use. More than half of the 510(k) submissions received by FDA have quality problems. Although FDA is meeting its performance goals for 510(k)s, these submission quality problems delay the completion of the marketing clearance process and unnecessarily divert resources from more productive activities in the review process.

Comparisons Between the FDA and the European Union

As FDA and industry have geared up to negotiate a new user fee agreement under MDUFA, we've seen reports and studies comparing FDA and EU [European Union] device review performance, with some suggesting that we replace the American system with that of the EU. It is important to note that there are some very basic differences between the two systems that confound comparisons. In contrast to the US medical device regulatory system, the European system:

- does not require government review before a company may market a device;
- does not require demonstration of device effectiveness— the US standard in law is safety and effectiveness; the EU standard is safety and performance, meaning the device must perform as indicated in the device description and is not required to show benefit to the patient;
- allows manufacturers to "forum-shop" their applications among third-party reviewers who are subject to minimal oversight;
- provides minimal information to the public about the evidence supporting company claims; for example, summaries describing the basis for third-party reviewer decisions to grant a CE [European quality control] mark are not provided to the public;
- has no centralized authority for tracking safety information related to medical devices and no EU-wide post-market surveillance system; as a result, the EU is less likely to detect new safety problems as compared to the United States; and
- has no centralized database of information about the performance of the various regulatory systems (such as time spent on premarket review) making it difficult to compare the performance of the EU and US systems.

Review Times Differ Between the United States and the European Union

In 2008, the European Commission acknowledged that there were limitations in its regulatory framework for medical devices and sought public comment on ways to strengthen its system. As noted by the Commission in its Public Consultation Report: "Experience indicates that the current system does not always offer a uniform level of protection of public health in the European Union. New and emerging technologies have challenged the current framework, highlighting gaps and pointing to a certain scarcity of expertise. . . . And finally, the legal system has been criticized as being too fragmented and difficult to follow and fraught with national variation."

Different studies report different time frames for US and EU review times for new medical devices, for a variety of reasons. Comparisons of review times between the United States and the EU are particularly difficult when based on flawed assumptions and in the absence of performance data for the EU. For example, the widely cited Makower study, which concluded there was a significant lag in "review times" in the United States as compared to the EU, included within the "review time" the substantial pre-submission assistance to the industry that FDA offers.

For the most complex devices, FDA reviews may indeed take longer from our first contact with a company to approval—in large part, due to our agreement with manufacturers to engage with them far earlier in the product development process than do our European counterparts. Of note, the number of such meetings requested by manufacturers has been steadily increasing over the past few years.

FDA Standards Are Tougher for High-Risk Devices

An additional factor is that for the higher-risk devices, FDA may ask for more robust clinical data to meet the stronger US regulatory standards. As noted previously, FDA requires a manufacturer to demonstrate that a device is safe and effective, while the European process only requires a demonstration of a device's safety and performance, not its effectiveness. For example, if a manufacturer wishes to market a laser to incise heart tissue to treat arrhythmia (abnormal heart rhythm) in the EU, the manufacturer must show that the laser incises heart tissue only. In the

US, however, the manufacturer must show that the laser incises heart tissue and also treats the arrhythmia.

Comparisons of safety data are equally problematic. Since the number of approval submissions or "on-market" devices in the EU cannot be determined from publicly available information—nor can the number of recalls or adverse event reports—calculation of accurate rates of safety problems is not possible. According to the industry-funded BCG study on EU and US recalls, 85 percent of medical device safety reports in the EU come from only five member states of the 24 countries reviewed, underscoring the potential for underreporting of safety events in the EU.

FDA Standards Have Protected US Citizens

We appreciate the concern that some devices come on the market in the EU before they do in the United States. While we want devices to be available to American patients as soon as possible, we believe that, consistent with US law, they need to be both safe and effective. The US system has served patients well by preventing EU-approved devices that were later shown to be unsafe or ineffective from harming American consumers. For example, in 1991, Poly Implant Prosthese (PIP), a company based in southern France, received a CE mark for silicone breast implants. Unbeknownst to regulators, PIP changed the silicone gel in the breast implants. On March 30, 2010, French regulators issued a recall of all pre-filled silicone breast implants manufactured by PIP. The breast implant recall is said to affect an estimated 35,000 to 45,000 women worldwide. This device was never approved by FDA and therefore never reached the market in the United States.

Yet, FDA recognizes that it can do a better job at managing its premarket review programs. FDA continues to look for ways to improve our ability to encourage innovation and to speed safe and effective products to patients. We know that medical device development is expensive. And we agree that in many areas, insufficient clarity, consistency, and predictability on our part contributes to those expenses. This is why we've undertaken initiatives to improve our review processes in order to enhance innovation in the medical device industry.

The FDA Voluntarily Investigates Its 510(k) Process

In recent years, concerns have been raised, both within and outside of FDA, about whether the current 510(k) program optimally achieves its goals of fostering innovation while making safe and effective medical devices available to patients. In light of these concerns, and in keeping with the good government practice of periodically assessing the effectiveness of existing programs, FDA launched in September 2009 a two-pronged, comprehensive assessment of the 510(k) process to determine whether changes should be made to the program so that it can better achieve its goals.

Under the first part of this assessment, FDA created two staff working groups—one to review the 510(k) program and make recommendations to strengthen it; the other, to review how the Agency incorporates new science into its decision-making process and recommends how it can do so more predictably. The other part of this assessment is an independent evaluation by the Institute of Medicine (IOM), which is still underway. The IOM is expected to publish its final report in summer 2011.

In keeping with our commitment to transparency, FDA sought public input during the development and review of the two internal reports. We engage in extensive public outreach, including two public meetings, three town hall meetings, three public dockets and many smaller meetings with a variety of stakeholder groups. In August 2010, FDA issued final reports containing 55 recommendations and again sought public comment on the reports and recommendations before taking action.

Revising the 510(k) Process

In January 2011, after reviewing the public comment, the Agency announced the actions it would take to improve the 510(k) process and its use of science in decision-making generally. In particular, these actions are intended to improve the predictability, consistency, and transparency of the 510(k) program and aspects of our PMA program, such as decisions regarding clinical trial protocols to facilitate innovation while assuring that devices available to patients are safe and effective. A few examples include:

- Streamlining the review process for innovative, lower-risk products, called the "de novo" classification process;
- Publishing guidance for industry to clarify when clinical data should be submitted to increase predictability and transparency;
- Developing a network of external experts who can use their knowledge and experience to help the Agency address important scientific issues regarding new medical device technologies; and
- Establishing a new Center Science Council of senior FDA experts within the Agency's medical device center to ensure more timely and consistent science-based decision-making.

The Innovation Pathway Program

In addition to our review of the 510(k) program, we recently announced a priority review program for new, breakthrough medical devices. The proposed new Innovation Pathway program for pioneering medical devices is part of a broader effort we have underway designed to encourage cutting-edge technologies among medical device manufacturers.

The Innovation Pathway will seek to accelerate the development and regulatory evaluation of innovative medical devices, strengthen the nation's research infrastructure for developing breakthrough technologies, and advance quality regulatory science. As part of this initiative, CDRH is proposing additional actions to encourage innovation, streamline regulatory and scientific device evaluation, and expedite the delivery of novel, important, safe and effective innovative medical devices to patients, including:

- Establishing a priority review program for pioneering technologies;
- Establishing a voluntary, third-party certification program for US medical device test centers, designed to promote rapid improvements to new technologies during a product's development and clinical testing stages;
- Creating a publicly available core curriculum for medical device development and testing to train the next generation of innovators; and
- Engaging in formal horizon scanning—the systematic monitoring of medical literature and scientific funding to predict where technology is heading, in order to prepare for and respond to transformative, innovative technologies and scientific breakthroughs.

Facilitating medical device innovation is a top priority for FDA. As part of its 2011 Strategic Plan, FDA's medical device center set goals to proactively facilitate innovation to address unmet public health needs. A public docket has been set up to solicit public comment on the Innovation Pathway proposals, and a public meeting on the topic is scheduled for March 15, 2011.

The Reauthorization of MDUFA

As you know, the statutory authority for MDUFA expires on September 30, 2012. At that time, new legislation will be required for FDA to continue collecting user fees for the medical device program. FDA is currently engaged in negotiations with the regulated industry to prepare recommendations for the reauthorization of MDUFA. In addition, the Agency is holding regular monthly discussions with representatives of patient and consumer advocacy groups, while the negotiations with industry are taking place, as required by the statute. Minutes of both the industry negotiations and the monthly stakeholder meetings are being made publicly available on the FDA website to ensure transparency of the reauthorization process and to facilitate stakeholder involvement in that process. Finally, FDA will hold a public meeting on MDUFA reauthorization later this year.

Issues of concern to industry will appropriately be addressed in these negotiations, and during this process, all other stakeholders—including the scientific and medical community, and patient and consumer groups—will be afforded the opportunity to make their views heard with respect to the reauthorization of MDUFA.

We look forward to working with Members of the Committee on Energy and Commerce to reauthorize this important legislation.

Mr. Chairman, I commend the Subcommittee's efforts to understand the impact of FDA's regulatory policies on medical device innovation. FDA strives toward a reasonable and fair approach to regulation that will foster innovation in the medical technology industry while assuring that the medical devices marketed in the United States are safe and effective. Thank you for your commitment to the mission of FDA, and the continued success of our medical device program, which helps get safe and effective technology to patients and practitioners on a daily basis.

Mr. Chairman, that concludes my formal remarks. I will be pleased to answer any questions the Subcommittee may have.

"Under current FDA processes, millions of U.S. patients are being denied or delayed access to leading medical devices that are first (or exclusively) brought to market in other countries."

Regulation of Medical Technology Delays US Patients' Access to Treatments

Josh Makower

In the following viewpoint, a medical professor presents findings from a survey he conducted that examined companies' experiences with the US Food and Drug Administration (FDA) medical device regulation process. He found that the process was much longer than in Europe and very expensive. The drawn out process means that US patients are denied access to the latest in medical treatments, the author explains. He contends that the United States will lose its place as global leader of medical technology if the FDA does not revise its regulatory process. Josh Makower is a consulting professor of medicine at Stanford University, CEO of ExploraMed Development, and partner at the venture capital firm NEA.

As you read, consider the following questions:

1. How many unique companies were surveyed as part of Makower's study and what percentage of the industry do they represent?
2. According to Makower, how many months on average did premarket approvals for high-risk devices take in the United States as compared to Europe?
3. What is the total cost of the regulatory process for low- to moderate-risk products in the United States, according to Makower?

Over the past few years, the manner in which the U.S. Food and Drug Administration (FDA) is executing its authority over the regulation of medical devices in the U.S. has been called into question. While some have claimed that current regulatory requirements are lax and harming patients, independent analysis has demonstrated that the current system does an exceptional job of protecting patients. However, with regard to the agency's objective of promoting the public health through new innovations, there are increasing concerns from patients, physicians, and innovators that the FDA is falling short. Until now, little (if any) data has been produced to either validate or refute these concerns.

Assessing the FDA's Regulatory Process

The purpose of this study was to address the need for data that could be used to evaluate the impact of U.S. medical device regulation on innovation and patients. The authors initiated the study in summer 2010 so that the results could be used to inform discussions underway within the FDA and the Institute of Medicine (IOM).

The U.S. regulatory system uses a combination of processes before a product is available to patients (referred to as the premarket period) and after a product has been cleared/approved for market (referred to as the postmarket period) to ensure patient safety and product effectiveness. The study, which took the form of a survey, focused exclusively on assessing premarket regulatory processes. It was used to help determine if concerns about the efficiency of current U.S. regulatory processes were isolated or widespread across the medical technology ("medtech") industry. It was also designed to identify where the greatest deterrents to innovation exist within U.S. premarket regulatory processes and the costs (in time and dollars) these issues place on U.S. medtech companies. This report summarizes the results of the study and explores the implications of the data on patients, innovators, the U.S. medtech industry, and the economy at large.

Responses from 204 unique companies are reflected in the study data. This number represents approximately 20 percent of all public and venture-backed medical device manufacturers in the U.S. that are focused on bringing innovative new technologies to market to improve the public health (e.g., devices used to treat hypertension, obesity). Survey participants were asked about their experiences in working with the FDA, as well as their experiences working with European regulatory authorities so that comparisons could be made between aspects of the two dominant regulatory systems that assure the safety of innovative technology in the global marketplace.

Survey Results for Low- and Moderate-Risk Devices

In general, survey respondents viewed current U.S. regulatory processes for making products available to patients (the premarket process) as unpredictable and characterized by disruptions and delays. For example, 44 percent of participants indicated that part-way through the premarket regulatory process they experienced untimely changes in key personnel, including the lead reviewer and/or branch chief responsible for the product's evaluation. A total of 34 percent of respondents also reported that appropriate FDA staff and/or physician advisors to the FDA were not present at key meetings between the FDA and the company. Factors such as these make the U.S. premarket regulatory process inefficient and resource intensive.

The above factors also contribute to significant delays in navigating FDA regulatory processes. Survey respondents reported that the premarket process for 510(k) pathway devices (of low- to moderate-risk) took an average of 10 months from first filing to clearance. For those who spoke with the FDA about conducting a clinical study for their low- to moderate-risk device before making a regulatory submission, the premarket process took an average of 31 months from first communication to being cleared to market the device. In contrast, respondents said it took them an average of 7 months in Europe from first communication to being able to market the same (or equivalent) device.

Survey Results for High-Risk Devices

For higher risk devices seeking premarket approvals (on the PMA pathway), responding companies indicated that it took an average of 54 months to work with the FDA from first communication to being approved to market the device. In Europe, it took an average of 11 months from first communication to approval.

The FDA compared unfavorably to European regulatory authorities in other ways, as well:

- *Predictability*: 85 percent of respondents considered EU authorities to be highly or mostly predictable, while only 22 percent gave the FDA the same ratings.

- *Reasonableness*: 91 percent of respondents rated EU authorities as highly or mostly reasonable compared to just 25 percent for the FDA.

- *Transparency*: 85 percent found the processes and decisions of the EU authorities to be highly or mostly transparent compared to 27 percent for the FDA.
- *Overall Experience*: 75 percent of respondents rated their regulatory experience in the EU excellent or very good. Only 16 percent gave the same ratings to the FDA.

Regulatory Costs Are Too High in the United States

The survey data also showed that the average total cost for participants to bring a low- to moderate-risk 510(k) product from concept to clearance was approximately $31 million, with $24 million spent on FDA dependent and/or related activities. For a higher-risk PMA product, the average total cost from concept to approval was approximately $94 million, with $75 million spent on stages linked to the FDA. (These estimates do not include the cost of obtaining reimbursement or any sales/marketing-related activities.) Survey respondents confirmed that they are able to make their products available to patients faster and at a significantly lower cost in markets such as Europe. For U.S. companies, these mounting costs are unsustainable in a venture-backed industry where less than one out of four medtech start-ups succeed, 50 percent of all reported exits are less than $100 million, and the total pool of available investment capital is shrinking.

Approval Takes Too Long in the United States

Perhaps most importantly, the survey revealed that the suboptimal execution of FDA premarket regulatory processes has a significant, measureable cost to U.S. patients in the form of a device lag. Respondents reported that their devices were available to U.S. citizens an average of two full years later than patients in other countries, due to delays with the FDA and/or company

We've heard that laughter is the best medicine, so beginning Monday we'll be regulating it.

"We heard that laughter is the best medicine . . . " cartoon by Douglas Pike. www.Car toonStock.com. Copyright © Douglas Pike. Reproduction rights obtainable from www .CartoonStock.com.

decisions to pursue markets outside the U.S. before initiating time-consuming, expensive regulatory processes in their own country. In some cases, this device lag reached up to 70 months (nearly six years).

The United States May Cease to Be a Global Leader in Medical Technology

Unpredictable, inefficient, and expensive regulatory processes put the U.S. at risk of losing its global leadership position in medtech innovation. Data from the survey clearly indicate that European regulatory processes allow innovators to make new medical technologies available to patients more quickly and at a lower cost. The reasonable question has been raised whether greater regulatory efficiency in the EU has been achieved at the expense of patient safety. However, no information is currently available to suggest that patient safety in Europe has been compromised. If the same devices become available in U.S. following their European approval only after extensive delays and additional costs are accrued, we must evaluate whether U.S. premarket regulatory processes are truly contributing to the advancement and promotion of the public health, or if they are actually restraining it.

Under current FDA processes, millions of U.S. patients are being denied or delayed access to leading medical devices that are first (or exclusively) brought to market in other countries. Fewer medical device start-ups are being launched in the U.S. as investment capital in the industry continues to move to other sectors. And, innovators and medical device companies are relocating to other countries in greater numbers, taking valuable jobs and tax revenue with them. Regulators and innovators must work together to reverse these troubling trends. To truly promote the public health, the FDA must impose reasonable regulatory requirements on new innovations, implement more balanced requirements for premarket and postmarket clinical data, and go back to leveraging market forces to reward technology that presents the greatest value to patients. Only then will the most effective advances in medical care be developed and provided promptly to American patients; and only then will the public health and our economy be best served.

> *"While many mobile medical apps don't pose any obvious risks to patients, it isn't always easy to separate the wheat from the chaff."*

Regulating Mobile Medical Apps Will Increase Their Utility and Availability

Tracy Granzyk Wetzel

In the following viewpoint, a journalist discusses the regulatory up-heaval that has occurred as the US Food and Drug Administration tries to catch up with the growing market of mobile medical apps. Despite the relatively low risk classification of most mobile medical apps, because some are used in determining diagnosis and treatment, they need regulation, she writes. According to the author, developers have found the regulatory process for mobile medical apps anything but smooth. Tracy Granzyk Wetzel is a Chicago-based writer specializing in health-care topics.

As you read, consider the following questions:

1. According to Wetzel, how many mobile health apps were available in the iTunes store as of February 2012?

2. As reported by Wetzel, what percentage of physicians used a mobile medical app for professional purposes in 2011?

3. What is the name of the initiative founded by the Healthcare Information and Management Systems Society to support mobile medical app developers as they go through the regulatory process, according to the author?

In July of 2011, the U.S. Food & Drug Administration (FDA) issued draft guidance around the regulation of mobile medical applications, and gathered comments through October.

While the intent of the guidance was to target a small group of mobile medical apps that turn mobile devices into diagnostic medical devices, it also raised questions—and concerns—about subjecting a rapidly evolving health information technology market to the arduous process that drug and medical device manufacturers have dedicated entire departments to managing since the 1938 Food, Drug and Cosmetics Act was enacted.

Today the iTunes store alone has approximately 9,000 consumer-focused mobile health applications and 4,000 targeted to health care professionals.

Those numbers are projected to grow to 13,000 and 6,000, respectively, this year provided the regulatory environment does not change drastically, according to Brian Dolan at mobihealth news.com.

The mobile medical apps for providers range from study aids for medical students, such as the USMLE [United States Medical Licensing Examination] Wiz 2 Flashcards by Current Clinical Strategies Publishing, to applications such as the ThinkLabs Stethoscope app, which is designed to enable a mobile device to capture and display heart and lung sounds, among other types of body sounds.

How the FDA Classifies Risk

In FDA-speak, medical devices, and now most likely their related mobile medical applications, are classified according to the risk they pose to the patient, and with greater risk comes greater regulatory potential.

Class I devices, such as an elastic bandage or exam gown, pose little risk to a patient. Class II devices, such as a glucose monitor or radiologic imaging device pose moderate risk and Class III devices, such as a drug eluting stent or intravascular catheter, pose the greatest risk to a patient if not manufactured according to best practice manufacturing standards.

Many of the Class I, and some of the Class II devices, are exempt from the FDA's Premarket Notification 510(k) process, but those that are not can submit a 510(k) if they are substantially equivalent (SE) to a legally marketed, or predicate device, not subject to a Premarket Application (PMA).

The cost of a 510(k) submission for FY [fiscal year] 2012, according to www.fda.gov, is $4,049, or $2,024 for a small business with less than $100 million in gross receipts or sales. Class III devices are most often subject to the PMA process, a more extensive and costly process when evaluating from the perspectives of time, money and manpower. The standard fee for a PMA in FY2012 is listed at $220,050, and $55,013 for a small business.

Evaluating Risk Level for Mobile Medical Apps

While many mobile medical apps don't pose any obvious risks to patients, it isn't always easy to separate the wheat from the chaff of what is now the growing crop of app developers and products entering the marketplace.

A medical student who is erroneously taught incorrect anatomy or medical Spanish via an app would most likely fail a test long before touching a patient. But developers entering the market with mobile medical apps that interpret X-ray findings, or calculate test results in order to diagnose or monitor patient information for treatment planning purposes, could have direct impact on patient care.

The FDA has stepped up to regulate this subset of medical apps. What remains unclear is which apps will fall under regulatory auspices and which will remain free of this additional cost burden to their business.

According to a 2011 study by Manhattan Research on the use of mobile devices and technology by U.S. physicians, 81 percent of the more than 2,000 survey respondents owned a smartphone in 2011, compared with 30 percent in 2010, and more than half used a mobile medical app for professional purposes in 2011, compared with one-third in 2010.

The FDA Regulatory Process Is No Smooth Ride

Mark Cain, chief technology officer at MIM Software Inc., has been through the FDA regulatory process with the company's MobileMIM application, and the process went anything but smoothly.

A journey that began in August of 2008 with its first 510(k) submission finally ended with FDA clearance on Feb. 4, 2011. The app provides mobile access to display SPECT [single-photon computed tomography], PET [position emission tomography], CT [computed tomography] or MRI [magnetic resonance imaging] scans for diagnostic purposes when a workstation is unavailable, and was presented in 2008 at Apple's World Wide Developers Conference where it was awarded the 2008 Apple Design Award for Best iPhone Healthcare & Fitness Application.

According to Cain, who has been developing software for medical imaging devices since 2002, MIM Software was already familiar with the regulatory process for medical devices, and was pretty certain the app would fall under the same regulations.

When radiologists who viewed the app confirmed their assumptions, MIM Software made plans to submit a 510(k).

"Unlike the average mobile medical app developer who may not know this world," says Cain, "we are medical device developers. We knew this would be used in the treatment and diagnosis of disease so we knew we could, and should, go to the FDA with a 510(k)."

The FDA Establishes Definitions for Mobile Medical Apps

In summary, the FDA draft guidance issued July 21, 2011, states that a "mobile medical app" is one that meets the definition of "device" in section 201(h) of the Federal Food, Drug, and Cosmetic Act and is either used as an accessory to a regulated medical device, or transforms a mobile platform (iPhone, Blackberry, iPad, etc.) into a regulated medical device.

The FDA defines a device as "an instrument, apparatus, implement . . . intended for the use in the diagnosis, cure, mitigation, treatment or prevention of disease in man, or intended to affect the structure or any function of the body of man or animal." And moving forward, disclaimers such as "not for diagnostic use" may not be enough to protect a developer from skirting regulatory responsibilities.

Cain puts it simply, "is it used in the treatment of, or diagnosis of disease? Period. End of story."

As Cain found, knowledge can be power but can also present obstacles others less aware avoid, at least in the short term.

The FDA Is Still Developing Its Approval Process for Mobile Medical Apps

As MIM Software traversed the approximately 29-month-long learning curve alongside the FDA, neither side found they were prepared for what the clearance of a mobile medical application would be like from a regulatory point of view.

When its first 510(k) submission was made in August of 2008, MobileMIM was deemed NSE, or not substantially equivalent, meaning the app was not deemed to be as safe or effective as the "predicate," i.e., an "equivalent" product already on the market.

A second 510(k) was filed in the summer of 2009 along with the additional data requested. And that is where the process broke down. For 221 days, the company heard nothing back from the FDA, and when it finally did, it was another rejection and a request for a PMA.

"At some point management changed, and an FDA ombudsman suggested we appeal the second 510(k), and forgo the request for the PMA-that this was not a Class III product," says Cain. "We added the calibration piece and performed additional testing and viewing with radiologists and resubmitted a third 510(k) in December of 2010." Approval came shortly thereafter, on Feb. 4, 2011, and Cain says the last 510(k) process was like night and day compared with the previous ones once the new reviewer stepped in.

The FDA Must Walk a Fine Line

"I wish it [the process] were less painful, but I also realize you don't want devices used that aren't approved," says Cain. "The FDA has a fine line to walk to provide the best impact for the industry given guidelines in relationship to timelines so that industry can plan. We had other products earning revenue so we could wait it out."

While they were inadvertently helping the FDA craft the clearance process for their industry, the industry went on doing its thing in the background. A number of imaging apps remained available for sale, labeled "not for diagnostic use" but similar to the ones commercially sold. "The rest of the industry has been moving ahead while we were going through the process," says Cain. "Not much has changed for other developers—it has been business as usual for them." However once the guidance is complete, this may change, Cain predicts, and the FDA may go back and clean up.

Bakul Patel, who currently holds the position of Policy Advisor in the Center for Devices and Radiological Health at the

FDA, understands very well the need to provide clarity and direction around how developers should proceed, especially those unfamiliar with medical device regulatory language.

In addition to holding an MBA, he is an electrical engineer by training, a Lean Six Sigma Black Belt and brings with him experience in fast paced, technology driven environments as a software engineer and manager.

"MIM Software already had a desktop viewer and was aware of the process, and we had been reviewing similar technology for a while," says Patel. "We now understand this area is growing quickly and need to rationalize where we need to be without compromising patient safety—thus the guidance. This example [MIM Software] led us to better understand what was needed."

The FDA Is Committed to Supporting Mobile Medical Apps

Patel says the FDA is committed to providing the appropriate level of oversight only to the narrow definition of the mobile medical apps as defined in the guidance.

For apps that meet the definition of medical devices per the guidance, the agency expects only a small number to submit for premarket clearance prior to marketing the app, and that the majority of apps would be considered Class I (low risk) devices and simply be required to register and list their products with the FDA.

"We are eager to support the continued development of mobile medical apps, without burdensome regulations that would stifle innovation," says Patel.

Patel is now busy sorting through 400, multiple-page comments in response to last year's proposed guidance, in order to finalize a guidance that makes sense for everyone—patients, users, manufacturers and developers—as soon as possible. Because of the volume of comments, Patel says that additional steps may be necessary before the final guidance is complete, sometime in 2012.

FDA Regulation of Mobile Medical Apps Is Nothing New

In a way, there is nothing "new" in the newly-released guidance from the FDA. Nothing new anyhow for companies that are well-experienced in delivering products and services subject to medical device regulations. . . . The only ones who will find anything "new" are entities who have up until now gratuitously denied that their health apps are medical devices subject to regulation . . . or validation testing or other SOPs [standard operating procedures] and controls of any kind.

Douglas S. McNair, "FDA Facing Huge Task in Regulating Mobile Medical Apps," www.cerner.com, August 9, 2011.

The 510(k) Process Improves

Mary Ellen Harrison, vice president of the HealthID division at PositiveID Corp., recently experienced the 510(k) process with iglucose, a mobile health system that aids diabetic patients in the management of their disease by transmitting data from compatible glucometers to a Web portal, allowing health care professionals access to their patients' information in real-time. She agrees that the 510(k) process is time consuming and requires dedicated effort and energy, but found the FDA to be very responsive to questions.

"It's a process that adds time and cost, but the end result is most important so that the consumer and health care provider can trust it [the iglucose system] works properly," says Harrison.

PositiveID filed its 510(k) in July of 2011 and was cleared by the FDA in November. All in all, it was a positive experience for the company, but Harrison says that its documentation was in order from the beginning and it dedicated both internal and external resources to the process, including engineers and other personnel who had worked with larger organizations on similar projects.

"You can't develop something like this in your garage," says Harrison. "If we didn't have a quality system and development process in place that we followed, there wouldn't be the same accountability."

The Regulatory Process Slows Innovation

While it's true that FDA regulations provide a check and balance system for medical-related products, it's the uncertainty around what the final guidance will look like that is leaving others less experienced with regulatory processes—but no less creative—on the sidelines, slowing the very innovation that could help solve today's health care woes, experts say.

Rebecca Kennis, a Systems Analyst from United Health Services health system in Johnson City, N.Y., has spent the last three years working on a hand-held version of its physician access application, called iCare.

Through iCare, physicians can securely access via iPhones both inpatient and outpatient data and view their census lists, patient labs, medications, ED [Emergency Department] reports, radiology transcription and sign-out notes. Kennis and her team, led by Afzal ur Rehman, M.D., a cardiologist with a love for computer programming, have also built in a billing component so that providers can not only input clinical information in real-time, but CPT [Current Procedural Terminology] codes and billing information as well.

"Even though iCare is view-only right now, we have received really good feedback from the physicians," Kennis says. "Providers like the fact that they can access this information from anywhere via their iPhone while they're on call. They can return a call from dinner, or right from their bed, and instantaneously receive information regarding their patient."

Complicating the Process

The next step for iCare would be to add decision support, such as alerts when labs or vitals indicate a potentially acute health issue.

But according to Kennis, adding those capabilities may be a regulatory game changer in the eyes of the FDA. "This is where things get gray."

After reading the guidance, Kennis says the company [is] in a holding pattern on adding the decision support as it waits to find out what the FDA will require.

"We're running a medical system off a medical device and we're not sure when the FDA needs to regulate. Right now its guidance appears contradictory—one section says clinical decision support falls under its regulatory guidance, and another section says [it doesn't]."

As a not-for-profit organization with limited manpower, Kennis hesitates to expand the iCare project in ways that may require FDA scrutiny because of the increased investment necessary to address the regulations.

The entire iCare project was developed by a three-person team, all of whom are also involved in a number of additional health system information technology and clinical projects, such as fulfilling meaningful use requirements, and in the case of Rehman, treating patients.

Because of its limited resources, UHS did not have time to send comments to the FDA about the regulatory guidance, and is relying in large part on industry associations like the Healthcare Information and Management Systems Society (HIMSS) to do so in its best interest, Kennis says.

Mobile Medical Apps Are Outpacing Regulation

Edna Boone, senior director of mHIMSS, the new mobile initiative the organization kicked off last year, says the pace at which mobile technologies are being adopted is outpacing organizational, national and international policies in place to regulate them.

HIMSS is focused on providing education around the new FDA guidance to its members, but would like the agency to provide more clarity about its intentions.

"We believe the FDA does understand its role in making sure outreach and education is out there," says Boone. "We would like to see them narrow their focus on the intended use, so we can better understand what needs to be regulated.

"This would help clarify things for those using the devices in hospitals and other health care settings."

In September of 2011, HIMSS polled its membership around the topic of mobile medical applications, and 243 members responded.

One-third of those responding felt the proposed FDA regulation was excessive, 41 percent believed the regulation to be appropriate and 6 percent felt additional regulation was necessary.

> *"While no system is perfect, without question, reliance on the FDA to protect America's health has proven a disastrous alternative in which corruption and industry bias overrides sound scientific judgment."*

Regulating Mobile Medical Apps Will Interfere with Patient Care

Jonathan Emord

In the following viewpoint, an attorney argues that the US Food and Drug Administration's (FDA) regulation of the mobile medical app market is stifling innovation and preventing people from receiving the best possible medical treatment. One of the biggest problems with the FDA's involvement in mobile medical apps, the author asserts, is the corrupt and biased nature of top officials within the FDA. The author claims these officials frequently skew science-based decisions to favor industry interests. He believes physicians are best positioned to judge what is safe and appropriate for a patient's care, not the FDA. Jonathan Emord is a writer and attorney who has tried several court cases against the FDA.

As you read, consider the following questions:

1. Which officials in the Center for Devices and Radiological Health were accused of misconduct in a whistleblower letter sent to the chairman of the House Energy and Commerce Committee in 2008, according to Emord?
2. After being trapped in regulatory limbo for two decades, what classification was the breast self-examination device Sensor Pad given, as described by Emord?
3. How are software upgrades to mobile medical apps handled by the FDA, according to Emord?

Mobile medical apps are prolific in the market. Created by physicians and scientists, most are used by physicians and hospitals to accelerate and reduce human error associated with computations needed for the use of various devices; to improve the quality of imaging used in diagnosis and treatment decisions; and to permit real time remote monitoring of cardiopulmonary functions, blood sugar levels, brain wave patterns, and numerous other indicia of disease. These innovations are vastly extending the reach of physicians and are greatly improving the lives, longevity, and freedom of patients. They are inextricably linked to medical practice which is evolving from hospital and clinic bound service to remotely delivered service. Having eyed the mobile medical app market since the 1980s, the FDA [US Food and Drug Administration] has now stepped forward to increase its regulatory presence—not through the legally required means of a rulemaking but through the autocratic alternative of an agency "guidance." Although characterizing its move into medical app regulation as limited, FDA's intervention threatens to politicize, retard, and disable a thriving and enormously beneficial marketplace.

As it has in every instance of market-wide regulation in the past, FDA now promises to regulate a huge part of the mobile medical app market and to determine within that market who may be a part of it and who may not, politically selecting winners and losers. Countless lives have been lost due to corruption, costly delays, and anticompetitive bias within the FDA's Center for Devices and Radiological Health (CDRH) and it is that center which will be primarily responsible for regulating mobile medical apps. As FDA endeavors to bring more and more mobile apps under its purview, ever increasing numbers of lives will be lost. What the market giveth, the government taketh away; and what the Lord giveth in life, the government taketh away also.

The FDA Begins Regulating Mobile Medical Apps

On July 21, 2011, FDA published its mobile medical app "guidance." While professing that it was engaged in a limited intervention into the market, the FDA in fact carved out an enormous universe to regulate: all mobile apps that function as accessories to existing medical devices; all mobile apps intended for use in the diagnosis of disease or other conditions or in the cure, mitigation, treatment, or prevention of disease; and all mobile apps intended to affect the structure or function of the body. It is scarcely possible to conceive of a medical app that would not be deemed a regulable device under FDA's regulatory definition.

In its guidance, FDA explains that a party that markets a mobile app meeting its definition is required to seek FDA approval, either in the form of a 510(k) substantial equivalence application (in which the applicant claims, rather absurdly, that its innovative app is substantially equivalent to an existing, FDA approved medical device) or in the form of a premarket approval application, carrying with it a whopping FDA filing fee of over $220,000.

Regulation Cools the Mobile Medical App Market

Aware that FDA can prosecute parties for selling mobile medical apps without FDA approval, many in the IT community who presently market such apps are contemplating getting out of the market and many who had planned to introduce new apps may avoid doing so. The effect will be to prevent the introduction of life saving and life enhancing technologies, destroy business and employment opportunities, and retard the development of a vibrant market in which physicians and hospitals serve as ensurers of patient safety, selecting only those apps that aid in the practice of medicine. Like all other FDA regulated markets, the mobile medical app market will become a dull market if the FDA succeeds in becoming the predominant player, the determining factor of market entry.

Without FDA regulation, physicians and hospitals do very well at protecting patient safety, albeit no system is perfect. Physicians are necessarily the primary determinants of the relative worth of a mobile medical app. That is as it should be because they are best situated to comprehend individual patient need and to appreciate the limitations of the technology. Substituting the FDA as an ultimate decision-maker invites political action to override sound medical judgment. FDA is in the business of catering to the needs of the largest medical device makers. For decades FDA's operational purpose has been to view the large industry players as its clients and to do their bidding, even if that means reversing the recommendations of career FDA scientists or, as in the case of Vioxx, countenancing the deaths of tens of thousands of Americans by defending the continued marketing of a bad drug.

FDA Officials Are Accused of Misconduct

The FDA has a long and sordid history of medical device regulation. In a letter sent to the then Chairman of the House Energy and Commerce Committee dated October 14, 2008, echoed in letters later sent in April of 2009 to President Obama, nine top FDA scientists complained of "misconduct" by FDA political managers in CDRH. The letter explained that those acts of misconduct reached "the highest levels of CDRH, including the Center Director [then Daniel G. Schultz] and the Director of the Office of Device Evaluation [then Donna-Bea Tillman]." The nine agency scientists explained that they possessed documentary evidence that CDRH political managers "corrupted and interfered with the scientific review of medical devices." In particular, they complained that CDRH political managers "ordered, intimidated and coerced FDA experts to modify their scientific reviews, conclusions and recommendations in violation of the law" and "ordered, intimidated and coerced FDA experts to make safety and effectiveness determinations that are not in accordance with scientific regulatory requirements, to use unsound evaluation methods, and [to] accept clinical and technical data that is not scientifically valid nor obtained in accordance with legal requirements, such as obtaining proper informed consent from human subjects." The letters explain that these same agency political managers avoided recording their orders and "engaged in reprisals and ignored . . . critical concerns" creating "an unwarranted risk to public health and a silent danger that may only be recognized after many years." Eerily, the letter confirms a horrible truth about the environment at FDA: "There is an atmosphere at FDA in which the honest employee fears the dishonest employee." FDA culture is one of political blame, defamation, and retribution.

Conflicts of Interest Inside the FDA

CDRH, like FDA in general, is ruled by political appointees. They are superior to every regulatory scientist at the agency. They make all final judgments issued by the agency, and they insinuate themselves into every aspect of scientific review. The personal financial and political interests of those appointees often conflict with outcomes dictated by sound scientific evaluations. For decades, medical reviewers in CDRH and the FDA Center for Drug Evaluation and Research (CDER) have often reached their wits end and have become whistleblowers, condemning the agency's leadership for being captives of leading industry and for

Regulation Will Drive Away Mobile Medical App Developers

Medical device manufacturers are fortunate to have experience with the FDA. On the other hand, app developers, many of whom are young, forward-looking entrepreneurs, do not; those who have already released products may find themselves unprepared, record-wise, for a strict FDA overhaul, while those still in development may otherwise redirect their approach to dodge regulation altogether.

Brady Donnelly, "While Healthcare Apps Are on the Rise, the FDA Threatens to Stifle Innovation in the U.S.," TNW Insider, June 9, 2012. www.thenextweb.com/insider.

doing that industry's bidding even at the expense of human life. That redundant testimony from dozens of scientists whose consciences have caused them to risk their own careers to warn the nation of an agency that knowingly approves unsafe drugs and devices is simple and profound: Inside FDA when political self-interest collides with science, political self-interest always wins.

When agency political appointees favor particular industry players by either helping to ensure that their applications are granted or by helping to ensure that regulatory obstacles remain in the path of those players' chief competitors, the appointees stand to benefit handsomely in post-government employment. Often those who leave the agency go to work for lobbying firms and are well compensated. Those firms in turn count as clients many of the same regulatees that have benefited from the decisions made by the political appointees when in office. This is quintessentially how Washington works and is an example of the pervasive bureaucratic corruption that has replaced individual sovereignty with bureaucratic oligarchy.

Industry Bias in the CDRH

The aforementioned nine top CDRH scientists' whistle blowing activity (combined with repeated accusations from within and without FDA that CDRH managers overruled science based decisions in favor of industry) created a fire storm surrounding two key figures within the CDRH political hierarchy, its Center Director Daniel B. Schultz and its Office of Device Evaluation Director Donna-Bea Tillman. Congressional heat, and pressure from groups like the Project on Government Oversight, ultimately became too great, producing a welcomed, albeit temporary, change of circumstances. CDRH Director Schultz resigned, professing that he did so for unrelated reasons, and CDRH Office of Device Evaluation Chief Tillman also resigned, likewise professing that she did so for unrelated reasons. Their fall from political grace did not cause them to land on rocky shoals, however. Schultz went on to become Senior Vice President for Greenleaf Health LLC, a "full service regulatory consulting firm that provides strategic guidance to companies regulated by the FDA," and Tillman went to become Director of Regulations and Policy at Microsoft Corporation's health information unit. Because the inherent financial incentives are so great for those FDA political appointees who will play the game of favoring key industry players, CDRH is now very much the same old politically biased beast that it was before the resignations.

The Impact of Regulatory Abuse on Breast Cancer

There are many examples of regulatory abuse of small, start-up companies that seek approval of their medical devices from the agency. Three examples will suffice to prove the point. In 1984 Don Perry of Decatur, Illinois, invented a means to enhance the sense of touch, enabling small irregularities on the surface of breast tissue to be sensed before the human hand would likely notice them. His invention was quite simple, two malleable pieces of plastic between which he sandwiched a silicon gel. The invention enabled self-breast examination to identify irregularities much earlier than direct tactile exams. This breakthrough in breast self-examination, the so-called Sensor Pad, held out the promise that people worldwide would be able to discover evidence of breast cancer long before they otherwise would, permitting them to alert physicians to the abnormalities and receive treatment if necessary. As we all know early detection of breast cancer greatly increases survival times and diminishes medical recommendations for radical mastectomies. How many people do we each know who realized too late that they had breast cancer and then suffered through a long, horrific ordeal ultimately ending in death? Both women and men can contract this deadly disease which is the second greatest cancer killer in women.

FDA Regulation at Its Worst

Thinking that no reasonable person could seriously question the safety or efficacy of their invention, Don Perry, Earl Wright and Earl's son Grant came to realize that the FDA was anything but reasonable. They soon realized that the FDA was a regulatory morass, a cesspool of corruption, red tape, and bias: the very antithesis of reason. They went through a decades long, circuitous regulatory odyssey at the agency, experiencing a seemingly endless deluge of inquiries which required that they provide costly responses, costing them millions and leaving Earl penniless. The penultimate example of FDA absurdity was a demand from CDRH that Earl provide proof of precisely how the device would lower the incidence of breast cancer, something any rational human being would know was impossible in advance of decades of actual marketing.

Ultimately, after severe criticism from members of Congress, the medical community, and the public, FDA opposition crumbled and the device was approved but not without a final regulatory slap: The device was approved as a high risk, heavily controlled item (Class III), requiring that it only be available by physician prescription. Thus, FDA approved the device over two decades after it was invented yet did so in a very narrow way, limiting its availability to physician prescription and thus ensuring that tens of millions of people worldwide would still not have access to it for daily breast self-examination and would still succumb to breast cancer that could have been detected before it became terminal.

An inestimable number of women who might otherwise have been saved from radical mastectomies or even death from breast cancer fell victim to those fates because of unreasonable FDA demands and delays. Likewise, with agency approval at Class III, an equally inestimable number of women still succumbed because of the all too common irrationality of America's foremost health agency.

A Breakthrough in Breast Cancer Radiation Treatment

Cleveland Clinic Chief Medical Physicist in the department of radiation oncology, Dr. Martin Weinhous, worked with colleagues to develop a medical software program that could transform measurements taken from a cancer infected breast and compute the precise x-ray positioning and dosing for radiation treatment. The software performed the calculations accurately within two minutes, avoiding underdosing and overdosing. Manual performance of the calculations required at least a half hour of physician time and was fraught with risk of error, oftentimes requiring that the recalculations be performed redundantly to reduce the risk of error. The software-generated guidance meant that people undergoing radiation treatment for breast cancer could avoid having inadequate radiation delivered to tumors and could also avoid having excessive radiation delivered to healthy tissue surrounding tumors. In short, while radiation is a horror, limiting its damage to non-cancerous tissue is certainly a major breakthrough.

Dr. Weinhous sought FDA approval for the software. He expected a reasonable review. Instead, he received inquiries that demanded so much time and money in proof that it became impossible for him to proceed. Indeed, the agency demanded that he prove that his software program would perform flawlessly on every conceivable PC and Macintosh configuration, an academic challenge that itself would require biomedical software engineers to develop highly sophisticated programs to address and would require numerous changes to the existing treatment software program, delaying introduction of the innovation for years and adding hundreds of thousands of dollars to the cost of development. Dr. Weinhous had no choice but to call it quits. Aware that his invention would save tens of thousands of women each year from harm, he nevertheless could not overcome the regulatory hurdles placed before him.

FDA Regulation Stifles Mobile Medical App Development

Even successful applicants are grossly hamstrung by FDA's regulatory labyrinth. Cleveland Case Western Biomedical Engineer Dennis Nelson shared other physicians' angst over just how difficult it was to read combined PET (positron emission tomography) and CT (computerized tomography) scans. Nelson then invented software that fused and enhanced combined PET, CT, and MRI (magnetic resonance imaging) scans, yielding a far superior image and thus improving diagnostic and treatment accuracy. The enhanced image appeared on iPhones and iPads, giving physicians the additional advantage of portability. Nelson and his new company MIM Software headed by CTO Mark Cain filed an application with the FDA seeking approval of the device. It took two and a half long and arduous years of effort and hundreds of thousands of dollars in expense before even this straight forward mobile medical app received approval. Moreover, the approval was limited to iPhone and iPad technology, thus excluding android technological applications. Moreover, the approval applies to the then existing program and not to more recent updates and modifications which, themselves, must be approved by FDA before used. Consequently, even FDA approval locks technological advance in a holding pattern. In an environment where software evolves daily and makes quantum leaps in evolution oftentimes every two to six months, the archaic FDA regulatory regime proves to be an impossibly formidable barrier, keeping America behind by locking innovation out of the marketplace.

The FDA Is Too Corrupt and Biased to Regulate Medical Technology

If we are to avoid FDA takeover of present and future medical practice, if we are to allow freedom enhancing and life saving technologies to reach patients before it is too late, and if we are to reap the many benefits of increased employment and prosperity that come from a free market in mobile medical application technology, we must remove FDA from the equation. The FDA has proven itself a corrupt tool of leading industry. It is structurally designed to have all decisions made politically and it is incapable of divesting politics from its decision-making. Even when it performs at its mediocre best, the FDA cannot keep pace with an exploding technological marketplace, one so innovative that each day brings with it a new development.

Moreover, the future of medical practice is inextricably linked to remote service. Besieged by patients whose illnesses work around the clock, physicians must take advantage of every efficiency and rely on the extraordinary power of mobile technologies to provide real time review of patient status and real time life saving intervention, regardless of the patient's location. This new technology not only enhances physician diagnostic and treatment accuracy but also liberates doctors and patients from hospital bedsides, enabling patients to enjoy greater freedom to obtain care away from the hospital and allowing the physician greater freedom to assist many more patients demanding his or her services.

Only if we get FDA out of the way and allow this extraordinary market to work can we reap the full benefits of the technology. Physicians have been and will continue to be the main line of defense for patients against faulty methods and treatments. While no system is perfect, without question, reliance on the FDA to protect America's health has proven a disastrous alternative in which corruption and industry bias overrides sound scientific judgment. We are far better off relying on physicians to care for their patients directly than relying on a distant, slow, and politically driven FDA to second guess every physician judgment about the best means to care for his or her patients.

Periodical and Internet Sources Bibliography

The following articles have been chosen to supplement the diverse views presented in this chapter.

Charlie Chi	"Which Way to Go: CE Mark or FDA Approval?," *Medical Design Technology*, February 7, 2012. www.mdtmag.com.
Paul Citron	"Medical Devices: Lost in Regulation," *Issues in Science and Technology*, vol. 27, no. 3, Spring 2011. www.issues.org.
Gregory Conko and Sam Kazman	"Recognize the Deadly Effects of Over-Regulating Medicines and Medical Devices," Competitive Enterprise Institute, December 21, 2010. www.cei.org.
Kenny Lin	"The Promise and Pitfalls of Medical Apps for Doctors," *U.S. News & World Report*, August 26, 2011. health.usnews.com.
Lawrence Miller	"US Regulatory Bodies Respond to Rapid Rise of Modern Wireless Technology and Apps for Medical Devices," *The Medical Technology Blog*, July 28, 2011. medical-technologyblog.com.
David Nexon	"A Delicate Balance: FDA and the Reform of the Medical Device Approval Process," Testimony before the Senate Special Committee on Aging, US Senate, April 13, 2011. aging.senate.gov.
Joel White	"FDA's Assault on Mobile Technologies," *Washington Times*, February 7, 2012. www.washingtontimes.com.
Anna Yukhananov	"Senators Propose Relaxing FDA Conflict Rules," *Reuters*, October 13, 2011. www.reuters.com.

For Further Discussion

Chapter 1

1. Would you undergo robotic surgery? What are the main points in favor of and against robotic surgery? Use the viewpoints from Roger Allan and Lisa Weidenfeld and Joseph Uchill to inform your answer. Which arguments do you find the most compelling and why?

2. Read the viewpoints by Emily Singer and Kent Bottles and reflect on their assessments of the utility of self-tracking. Given the cost and the time that goes into self-tracking, do you think it is a worthwhile endeavor? Why or why not? If not, what should people do instead?

Chapter 2

1. Some people argue, as does the Kaiser Family Foundation, that new medical technology contributes to rising costs in health care. Do you agree or disagree with this view? Why or why not? What are three solutions that you can think of to address the issue of rising medical expenses?

2. Do you agree with Sean R. Tunis et al. that giving the Centers for Medicare and Medicaid Services more leeway to conduct its own research and review of medical technology would help control health-care costs? Why or why not?

Chapter 3

1. EMRs have been touted as a way for medical offices and hospitals to become more efficient. After reading the viewpoints by Bernie Monegain and Alexi Mostrous, do you think EMRs will eventually reduce or increase errors? What other problems or benefits do you as a health-care consumer see that may not have been mentioned in the viewpoints?

2. In terms of security, EMRs have both benefits and down-sides as compared to traditional paper records. Which type of medical record would you prefer? Do you maintain an electronic health record—a personally maintained record of your medical information? After reading the viewpoints by Liv Osby and Linda Thede, do you think your health information is more or less secure? If you answered less, what steps do you think need to be taken to make the information more secure? Is medical identity theft a real concern for you? Why or why not?

Chapter 4

1. The regulation of medical devices is a hotly contested aspect of public policy because of the money involved for both the industry and the FDA. After reading the viewpoints by Jeffrey Shuren and Josh Makower, do you think the FDA is doing the best it can to provide a fast, but thorough review of applications? Industry advocates argue that regulation in Europe is more efficiently handled. Do you think medical devices in Europe are as carefully reviewed, given the faster turnaround? Do you think patients in the United States suffer as a result of the FDA's slower approval process?

2. Mobile medical applications in the hands of doctors can have a direct impact on patient health, and the FDA is stepping in to regulate these apps in an effort to protect the public health. Do you think the FDA is making too much of the impact that mobile medical apps will have on medical treatment? How much regulation of mobile medical apps do you think is needed to keep people safe? Some argue that regulating apps suppresses innovation and denies care for people who could have benefitted from an app. Do you think this is a real concern? App developers who are not particularly focused on the health-care industry are turning toward other projects to avoid dealing with the lengthy regulation

process. Is this good or bad? Do you think the FDA should make mobile medical app regulation a faster process or do the drawbacks outweigh the benefits? Use the viewpoints by Tracy Granzyk Wetzel and Jonathan Emord to support your answers.

Organizations to Contact

The editors have compiled the following list of organizations concerned with the issues debated in this book. The descriptions are derived from materials provided by the organizations. All have publications or information available for interested readers. The list was compiled on the date of publication of the present volume; names, addresses, phone and fax numbers, and e-mail and Internet addresses may change. Be aware that many organizations take several weeks or longer to respond to inquiries, so allow as much time as possible.

Advanced Medical Technology Association (AdvaMed)
701 Pennsylvania Avenue NW, Suite 800
Washington, DC 20004-2654
(202) 783-8700
e-mail: info@advamed.org
website: www.advamed.org

The Advanced Medical Technology Association is a professional association for developers of medical technology, representing 90 percent of medical device manufacturers in the United States and 50 percent globally. AdvaMed advocates for its members on legal, economic, and regulatory issues. It publishes the *Medical Technology Investment Digest* and numerous briefs and news reports.

Centers for Disease Control and Prevention (CDC)
1600 Clifton Road
Atlanta, GA 30333
800-CDC-INFO
e-mail: cdcinfo@cdc.gov
website: www.cdc.gov

A division of the United States Department of Health and Human Services, the Centers for Disease Control and Prevention is the nation's premier public health organization. The mission of the CDC is "to promote health and quality of life by preventing and controlling disease, injury, and disability." The CDC website provides fact sheets, publications, news articles, and statistics about infectious disease, including a 2009 special report on medical technology in the United States. Sample publications include *Emerging Infectious Diseases; Morbidity and Mortality Weekly Report*; and *Adolescent and School Health.*

Center for Integration of Medicine and Innovative Technology (CIMIT)

165 Cambridge Street, Suite 702
Boston, MA 02114
(617) 643-3800
website: www.cimit.org

The Center for Integration of Medicine and Innovative Technology seeks to improve patient care through interdisciplinary collaborative research. It provides resources for innovative research to clinicians, engineers, and scientists who are part of its consortium of institutions, as well as workshops, classes, and grants. News and video about CIMIT-sponsored work is available on its website.

Healthcare Information and Management Systems Society (HIMSS)

33 West Monroe Street, Suite 1700
Chicago, IL 60603-5616
(312) 664-4467
website: www.himss.org

Healthcare Information and Management Systems Society is a non-profit, global organization that provides information and leadership in the field of health-care information technology. In addition to hosting conferences around the world, HIMSS provides professional development, research initiatives, and disseminates information through various media vehicles, including its website. Various publications produced by HIMSS are available on its website, including *Healthcare IT News.*

Medical Technology and Practice Patterns Institute (MTPPI)
4733 Bethesda Avenue, Suite 150
Bethesda, MD 20814
(301) 652-4005
website: www.mtppi.org

Medical Technology and Practice Patterns Institute is a non-profit organization that seeks to better inform public policy surrounding medical technology. The institute researches "the clinical and economic implications of health care technologies" using clinical studies, longitudinal analysis, patient outcomes, and other avenues of investigation. Its findings are publishing in peer-reviewed journals or on the institute's website.

National Coalition on Health Care
1030 15th Street NW, Suite 690 West
Washington, DC 20005
202-638-7151
e-mail: info@nchc.org
website: www.nchc.org

The National Coalition on Health Care is an advocacy organization committed to the need for comprehensive health-care reform in the United States. The organization's website provides articles and full-text speeches about the state of health care, health-care information technology, drug and device cost containment, innovation, and safety. In addition, the group also offers important data bulletins, including "Physician Ownership of Medical Equipment," which discusses problems with doctors who overuse equipment that they own.

National Institutes of Health (NIH)
9000 Rockville Pike
Bethesda, MD 20892

(301) 496-4000
e-mail: NIHinfo@od.nih.gov
website: www.nih.gov

The National Institutes of Health is the medical research agency of the United States. The NIH provides consumer health information as well as information about clinical trials on its website. In addition, the website features relevant news stories as well as both audio and video programming.

National Patient Safety Foundation

268 Summit Street, 6th Floor
Boston, MA 02210
(617) 391-9900
e-mail: info@npsf.org
website: www.npsf.org

The National Patient Safety Foundation is a non-profit advocacy group dedicated to improving patient safety. Its website includes information on surgical errors, medication errors, falls, and diagnostic errors, among others areas of patient safety. The foundation provides online courses, fact sheets, white papers, and tools for both physicians and patients.

World Health Organization (WHO)

Avenue Appia 20 1211
Geneva 27 Switzerland
41-22-791-21-11
e-mail: info@who.int
website: www.who.int

The World Health Organization is the directing and coordinating authority for health of the United Nations. As such, WHO is a global force in health care. The WHO website includes multimedia presentations, fact sheets, news articles, publications, brochures and statistics. The website also offers e-books and information on ordering materials through the mail.

US Food and Drug Administration (FDA)

10903 New Hampshire Avenue
Silver Spring, MD 20993
(888) INFO-FDA
website: www.fda.gov

The FDA is responsible for consumer safety in the United States. Its Center for Devices and Regulatory Health (CDHR) protects the public health through the regulation of medical devices. The CDHR also collects information on device safety and recall, including those that emit radiation. The FDA's medical device regulation website has up-to-date lists of device recalls, radiation-emitting products, and approved medical devices.

Bibliography of Books

George M. Burnell

Final Choices: To Live or to Die in an Age of Medical Technology. New York: Insight Books, 1993.

Daniel Callahan

Taming the Beloved Beast: How Medical Technology Costs Are Destroying Our Health Care System. Princeton, NJ: Princeton University Press, 2009.

Ruth Chadwick, ed.

The Concise Encyclopedia of the Ethics of New Technologies. San Diego: Academic Press, 2001.

Amiram Daniel and Edward Kimmelman

The FDA and Worldwide Quality System Requirements Guidebook for Medical Devices, second ed. Milwaukee: ASQ Quality Press, 2008.

Carl T. DeMarco

Medical Device Design and Regulation. Milwaukee: ASQ Quality Press, 2011.

Richard A. Deyo

Hope or Hype: The Obsession with Medical Advances and the High Cost of False Promises. New York: AMACOM, 2005.

Richard C. Fries

Reliable Design of Medical Devices, second ed. Boca Raton, FL: CRC Press, 2006.

William Hanson

The Edge of Medicine: The Technology That Will Change Our Lives. New York: Palgrave Macmillan, 2009.

Gordon Harnack — *Mastering and Managing the FDA Maze: Medical Device Overview.* Milwaukee: ASQ Quality Press, 1999.

Philip J. Hilts — *Protecting America's Health: The FDA, Business, and One Hundred Years of Regulation.* New York: Knopf, 2003.

Anupam B. Jena and Tomas J. Philipson — *Innovation and Technology: Adoption in Health Care Markets.* Washington, DC: AEI Press, 2008.

Theodore R. Kucklick, ed. — *The Medical Device R&D Handbook*, second ed. Boca Raton, FL: CRC Press, 2006.

Patrick Kullmann — *The Inventor's Guide for Medical Technology: From Your Napkin to the Market.* Minneapolis: Two Harbors Press, 2012.

Robert L. Martensen — *A Life Worth Living: A Doctor's Reflections on Illness in a High Tech Era.* New York: Farrar, Straus, and Giroux, 2008.

Shreefal S. Mehta — *Commercializing Successful Biomedical Technologies: Basic Principles for the Development of Drugs, Diagnostics and Devices.* New York: Cambridge University Press, 2008.

Robert Mulcahy — *Medical Technology: Inventing the Instruments.* Minneapolis: Oliver Press, 1997.

Douglas Mulhall	*Our Molecular Future: How Nano-technology, Robotics, Genetics and Artificial Intelligence Will Transform Our World.* Amherst, NY: Prometheus Books, 2002.
Ramez Naam	*More Than Human: Embracing the Promise of Biological Enhancement.* New York: Broadway, 2005.
Suzanne Robitaille	*The Illustrated Guide to Assistive Technology and Devices: Tools and Gadgets for Living Independently.* New York: Demos Medical, 2010.
Robert Sneddon	*Medical Technology.* London: Evans Brothers, 2008.
Eric Topol	*The Creative Destruction of Medicine: How the Digital Revolution Will Create Better Health Care.* New York: Basic, 2012.
Peter A. Ubel	*Pricing Life: Why It's Time for Health Care Rationing.* Cambridge, MA: The MIT Press, 2000.
Terri Wells	*Medical Device Marketing: Strategies, Gameplans and Resources for Successful Product Management.* Parker, CO: Outskirts Press, 2010.
Elaine Whitmore	*Development of FDA-Regulated Medical Products: Prescription Drugs, Biologics, and Medical Devices.* Milwaukee: ASQ Quality Press, 2003.

Trenor Williams and Anita Samarth	*Electronic Health Records for Dummies*. New York: Wiley, 2010.
Anthony B. Wolbarst	*Looking Within: How X-Ray, CT, MRI, Ultrasound, and Other Medical Images Are Created, and How They Help Physicians Save Lives*. Berkeley: University of California Press, 1999.
Stefanos Zenios, Josh Makower, and Paul Yock	*Biodesign: The Process of Innovating Medical Technologies*. New York: Cambridge University Press, 2009.

Index

physician care, 28–29
research on value, *27*
technology creep and, 87
trauma reduction, 22–23
as worthy of costs, 29–30
See also Minimally invasive
surgical techniques; Robotic
surgery
Medicare
avoidance of unnecessary procedures, 111–112
biomedical perspective shift,
122
claim processing and, 117
coverage and payment policy
revisions needed, 117–118
coverage policy can be repaired,
118–119
coverage policy uneven,
119–120
doctors' services and, 111
future, 125
hospital bonuses, 143
improvements needed, 121
medical technology adds to
costs, 108–114
medical technology can contain
costs, 115–125
national coverage reviews
needed, 122–123
overview, 109–110, 116–117
patient care costs, 31
research priorities, 123–124
robotic surgery and, 49
spending control as controversial, 120–121
spending increases, 110–111
statutory authorities would
strengthen, 124–125
"Triple Aim," 118
Medicare Australia, 106

Medscape Hematology-Oncology
(online journal), 138
Medtronic (MDT), 133
Mexico, 130
Microsoft Corporation, 203
Migraines, 55, 60, 61
MIM Software Inc., 189–190, 192,
206
Minimally invasive surgical tech-
niques, 21, 22–23, 31–32
See also Robotic surgery
Mobile medical apps
complexity, 195
development outpacing regula-
tion, 195–196
evaluating risks of, 188–189
FDA regulations, 186–196,
199–208
overview, 187, 198–199
regulation interferes with pa-
tient care, 197–208
regulatory process difficulties,
189–190
risk classification and, 188
support, 192
MobileMIM app, 189, 190–191
Mohr, Penny E., 115–125
Molyneux, D.H., 24–25
Monegain, Bernie, 140–144
Moodscope, 68
Morbidity rates, 23, 45, 116
Morris, Skip, 154
Mortality rates, 15, 25, 35, 106, 116
Mostrous, Alexi, 145–150
The Motley Fool (company), 87
Motor Vehicle Manufacturers
Association, 135

N
Natale, Patricia, 141
National Academy of Sciences, 62,
74, 75

CPSIA information can be obtained
at www.ICGtesting.com
Printed in the USA
FFOW031206220213